GUIDE TO
MANAGERIAL
COMMUNICATION

GUIDE TO MANAGERIAL COMMUNICATION

second edition

MARY MUNTER

Amos Tuck School of Business
Dartmouth College

Prentice-Hall, Inc., *Englewood Cliffs, New Jersey 07632*

Library of Congress Cataloging-in-Publication Data

MUNTER, MARY.
    Guide to managerial communication.

    Bibliography: p. 158
    Includes index.
    1. Communication in management. I. Title.
II. Title: Managerial communication.
HF5718.M86 1987   658.4'5   86–9369
ISBN 0–13–370271–5

Editorial/production supervision and
    interior design: Joan L. Stone
Cover design: Photo Plus Art
Manufacturing buyer: Ed O'Dougherty

Printed in the United States of America

10 9 8 7

Quotation in Chapter I from Gunning, R., *More Effective Writing in Business and
Industry.* Boston: Industrial Education Institute, 1962, pp. 3, 11. Quotations in
Chapter II from Ewing, D., *Writing for Results in Business, Government, the Sciences,
and the Professions,* 2nd ed. New York: John Wiley, 1979, pp. 38–39 and 49–50; from
Flower, L., *Problem-Solving Strategies for Writing.* New York: Harcourt Brace
Jovanovich, 1981, pp. 86–87. Quotations in Chapter III from Wydick, R. "Plain
English for Lawyers," *California Law Review,* 66 (1978), p. 752; from Orwell, G.,
"Politics and the English Language," *Horizon,* 76 (April, 1946), pp. 252+, by
permission of the Estate of the late George Orwell.

ISBN 0-13-370271-5   01

PRENTICE-HALL INTERNATIONAL (UK) LIMITED, *London*
PRENTICE-HALL OF AUSTRALIA PTY. LIMITED, *Sydney*
PRENTICE-HALL CANADA INC., *Toronto*
PRENTICE-HALL HISPANOAMERICANA, S.A., *Mexico*
PRENTICE-HALL OF INDIA PRIVATE LIMITED, *New Delhi*
PRENTICE-HALL OF JAPAN, INC., *Tokyo*
PRENTICE-HALL OF SOUTHEAST ASIA PTE. LTD., *Singapore*
EDITORA PRENTICE-HALL DO BRASIL, LTDA., *Rio de Janeiro*

CONTENTS

For Paul

INTRODUCTION

HOW THIS BOOK CAN HELP YOU

The thought of giving that presentation next week is making you nervous. What can you do to relax?

You suddenly realize that you have written an entire single-spaced page consisting of two sentences. How can you break them into shorter, sharper, and more effective units?

In making your case, you don't know whether to start with your recommendation or to build up to it. Which is more persuasive?

You want to illustrate how your division ranks. What kind of chart would demonstrate ranking most effectively?

You seem to freeze up when it comes to writing that big report. How can you avoid writer's block?

What can you do about such problems? Turn to relevant parts of this book for guidance.

You would like to have a step-by-step procedure for preparing a written document or an oral presentation.

You would like a checklist for editing your writing carefully or for improving your speaking delivery.

What can you do? Read through this entire book for general procedures and techniques.

You know you are a good communicator; if you weren't, you would not be where you are now. You would like, however, to polish and refine your writing and speaking skills.

What can you do? Use this book in a professional training course, a college course, a workshop, or a seminar.

WHO CAN USE THIS BOOK

This book is written for people who need to write and speak in the business, government, and professional worlds—people, that is, who provide a service (in such fields as banking, law, consulting, or education) or a product (in such fields as manufacturing, marketing, finance, research, development, or engineering). This book is aimed at anyone who achieves results through directing, supervising, instructing, inspiring, persuading, or leading other people—anyone, that is, who necessarily relies on managerial communication.

If you are a business or professional manager, you probably already understand these important facts about your career and your managerial world:

About your career:

1. You spend most of your working time communicating (various studies estimate the amount at 50 to 90 percent).
2. Your career advancement definitely depends on your ability to communicate well (various surveys verify this conclusion, including those by the *Harvard Business Review, Fortune,* and the American Management Association).

About your managerial world:

1. Recent trends—for example, increased geographical distribution of companies, increased specialization, and increased numbers of pressure groups, such as consumers, labor, and government—make clear, persuasive communication more crucial than ever.
2. Recent developments in the electronic communication field—for example, telecommunications, text handling, data-base and filing systems, and data analysis—offer you the opportunity to communicate more often and more efficiently today.

WHY THIS BOOK WAS WRITTEN

From the thousands of participants in various business and professional speaking and writing courses I have taught, I have heard requests for a brief summary of communication techniques. Many busy professional people have found other books on communication skills too long, insultingly remedial, or full of irrelevant information.

This book is appropriate for you if you want a summary that is:

Short:

The book summarizes concisely results and models culled from thousands of pages of text and research. I have omitted bulky examples, cases, footnotes, and exercises.

Professional:

The book includes only information that professionals will find useful. You will not find instructions for study skills, such as in-class writing and testing; secretarial skills, such as letter typing and telephone answering; artistic skills, such as dialogue writing and dramatic reading; or job-seeking skills, such as résumé writing and job interviewing.

Readable:

I have tried to make the book clear and practical. The format makes it easy to read and to skim. The tone is direct, matter-of-fact, and non-theoretical.

HOW THIS BOOK IS ORGANIZED

The information on communication strategy in Chapter I applies to both writing and speaking: how to formulate your objectives, analyze your audience, structure your message, and choose your communication channel. This chapter presents basic strategies that are used throughout the rest of the book. The book then divides into two sections: writing and speaking.

The writing section covers both the writing process and the written product. Chapter II explains the process: (1) how to compose efficiently by generating material, organizing material, drafting, editing, and avoiding writer's block; and (2) how to select formats, including highlighting and business conventions. Chapter III describes the characteristics of an effective written "product": the document itself and its paragraphs, sentences, and words.

The speaking section also covers both the process and the product. Chapter IV delineates the process of preparing for presentations and other kinds of business-speaking situations and discusses content and equipment for visual aids. Chapter V describes the physical characteristics of good speaking: how to practice and make necessary arrangements; relax and gain confidence; and improve your delivery.

The last section of the book is for reference. Refer to Chapter VI for information on usage and punctuation. Refer to the bibliography in that chapter for the sources of my quotations and ideas or for further information on any topic I have discussed. For example, earlier in this introduction I alluded to surveys showing that managers spend most of their time communicating and to the importance of communication for career advancement. If you want documentation or further information on these claims—or others throughout the book—you can find it in the bibliography.

GUIDE TO MANAGERIAL COMMUNICATION

I

OUTLINE
COMMUNICATION STRATEGY

I. Writer/speaker strategy
   1. What are your objectives?
   2. What managerial style do you choose?
   3. What is your credibility?

II. Audience analysis strategy
   1. What do you know about your audience?
   2. How can you motivate your audience?

III. Message structure strategy
   1. What do you want to emphasize?
   2. Is your audience likely to agree, interested in results, very busy?
   3. Is your audience likely to disagree, interested in analysis?

IV. Channel choice strategy
   1. Writing
   2. Speaking

I

COMMUNICATION STRATEGY

Effective managerial communication is communication, written or spoken, that gets the response you desire from your audience. Therefore, before you start writing or speaking you should always set your communication strategy: (1) delineate your objectives, style, and credibility; (2) analyze the people in your audience and how to motivate them; (3) structure your message appropriately for your audience; and (4) choose the correct communication channel.

These four steps may seem simple and obvious, yet by remembering to take them you can avoid most of the speaking and writing problems that hamper clear communication in business and the professions today—problems such as unclear, unread memos or confusing, misunderstood presentations. This four-step model for communication strategy, then, codifies crucial information—information you may already know intuitively—about how to get the response you desire from your audience.

I. WRITER/SPEAKER STRATEGY

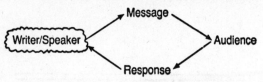

The first step in setting a communication strategy consists of decisions regarding yourself (the writer or speaker): analyzing your objectives, choosing your managerial style, and enhancing your credibility.

1. What are your objectives?

Defining your objectives provides two important benefits. First, you will be more efficient, because you will no longer waste time writing or presenting material unless you have a clear reason for doing so. Second, you will be more effective, because formulating your objective precisely will help you communicate more clearly.

The time needed to define your objectives varies: routine matters may take only seconds, more complex matters may take much longer.

To clarify your purpose, hone down your objectives from the general to the specific.

General objectives   These are your broad goals, the ones that trigger the creative process and start you thinking. They are comprehensive statements about what you are doing, what you hope to be doing, or what problem you are trying to solve.

Action objectives   To define your objectives more specifically, determine your action objectives—specific, measurable, time-bound steps that will lead toward your general objectives. State your action objectives in this form: "to accomplish a specific result by a specific time."

Communication objective   Your communication objective is even more specific. Based on your action objectives, decide precisely how you hope your audience will respond to your specific written or oral communication. To define your communication objective, complete this statement: "As a result of this communication, my audience will
_____."

EXAMPLES OF OBJECTIVES

General	Action	Communication
Provide mail service throughout the organization.	Pick up mail X times per X time period.	As a result of this memo, the mail delivery staff will follow the procedures delineated.
Increase customer base.	Contract with at least X number of clients per X time period.	As a result of this letter, the client will sign the contract.
Develop a sound financial position.	Maintain annual debt-to-equity ratio no greater than X.	As a result of this phone call, the accountant will give me the pertinent information for my report.
		As a result of this report, the Board will approve my recommendations.
Increase number of women hired.	Hire X number of women by X date.	As a result of this presentation, the supervisors will meet with their staffs to discuss this issue, reconvening later to determine a strategy.
		As a result of this presentation, at least X number of women will sign up to interview with my organization.
Increase market share.	Sell X amount by X date.	As a result of this memo, my boss will approve my implementation plan.

2. What managerial style do you choose?

In addition to specifying your objective, decide on the managerial style you want to use for the occasion—that is, how much control you want to maintain over your content and how much you want to involve your audience. Naturally, the more you control, the less you involve; the more you involve, the less you control. The following model, adapted from organizational behavior theorists Tannenbaum and Schmidt, displays the range of managerial styles:

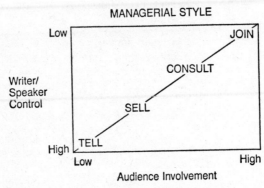

In the TELL (or inform) style, you want your audience to learn.

In the SELL (or persuade) style, you want your audience to act.

In the CONSULT (or interact) style, you want both yourself and your audience to learn.

In the JOIN (or collaborate) style, you want both yourself and your audience to act.

Your managerial communication style should vary with each situation you encounter. Generally, use tell/sell styles when you: (1) have sufficient information, (2) can understand that information without help from others, and (3) are concerned primarily with the quality of the decision. With these styles, a decision is more likely to be logical, orderly, and quick. Generally, use the consult/join styles when you: (1) need more information, (2) need critical evaluation from others, and (3) are concerned primarily with implementation. With these styles, a decision is more likely to be carried out effectively. (See the bibliography in Chapter VI for proponents of each of the four styles.)

EXAMPLES OF COMMUNICATION OBJECTIVES
AND MANAGERIAL STYLES

Communication objective	Managerial style	
As a result of reading this memo, the mail delivery staff will follow the procedures delineated. As a result of reading this report, my supervisor will understand the extent of last month's activities in my division.	**TELL**	In these situations, you are instructing or explaining. You do not need audience involvement. You want your audience to learn something.
As a result of reading this letter, the client will sign the contract. As a result of attending this presentation, my staff will understand the benefits of our controversial new policy.	**SELL**	In these situations, you are persuading. You need some audience involvement in order to do so. You want your audience to act.
As a result of reading this report, the Board will approve the changes suggested in the Recommendations section. As a result of this conference call, my clients will list what they want us to accomplish on project X.	**CONSULT**	In these situations, you are conferring. You cannot simply state or sell your content because you need your audience's opinions. You yourself need to learn.
As a result of attending this presentation, the supervisors will meet with their staffs to discuss this issue, reconvening later to determine a strategy. As a result of attending this presentation, the training staff will design a new course in sales techniques.	**JOIN**	In these situations, you are collaborating. You need very high audience involvement to discover your content. Both you and your audience will act.

3. What is your credibility?

Once you have formulated what you want to accomplish (that is, stated your objective and chosen the appropriate managerial style to accomplish it), consider your audience's perception of you. In other words, consider your own credibility: their belief, confidence, and faith in your power or reliability or trustworthiness. Their expectations of you have a tremendous impact on how you set your communication strategy.

Five factors—based on the research of social power theorists French, Raven, and Kotter—affect your credibility: (1) rank, (2) goodwill, (3) expertise, (4) image, and (5) fairness. Once you understand these factors, you can enhance your credibility by stressing your initial credibility and increasing your acquired credibility.

Initial credibility   The phrase "initial credibility" refers to your audience's perception of you before you even begin to communicate, before they ever read or hear what you have to say. Your initial credibility, then, may stem from their perception of who you are, what you represent, or how you have related to them previously.

As part of your communication strategy, you may want to stress or remind your audience of your initial credibility. Also, in those lucky cases in which your initial credibility is high, you may use it as a "bank account." If people in your audience regard you highly, they may trust you even in unpopular or extreme decisions or recommendations. Just as drawing on a bank account reduces your bank balance, however, drawing on your initial credibility reduces your credibility balance; remember to "deposit" to your account, perhaps by goodwill gestures or with further proof of your expertise.

Acquired credibility   "Acquired credibility," unlike initial credibility, refers to your audience's perception of you after the communication takes place, after they have read or heard you. Even if your audience knows nothing about you in advance, your good ideas and your persuasive writing or speaking will help you earn credibility. The obvious way to acquire credibility, therefore, is to do a good job analyzing and communicating in general.

You can, however, also use more specific communication techniques to increase your credibility. The following page lists these techniques.

EXAMPLES OF CREDIBILITY

Factor	Based on	Initial credibility Stress by	Acquired credibility Increase by
Rank	Hierarchical power	Emphasizing your title or rank (e.g., including your full title)	Associating yourself with high-ranked person (e.g., by countersignature or introduction)
Goodwill	Their best interests; personal relationships	Referring to personal relationships	Citing benefits or ideas that match your audience's goals and needs
Expertise	Knowledge; competence	Including a biography, résumé, or list of experience	Associating yourself with or quoting from someone your audience sees as expert
Image	Attractiveness; desire to be like you	Emphasizing attributes that your audience finds attractive	Identifying yourself with benefits or ideas that match your audience's goals and needs
Fairness	Values; standards	Mentioning values you share with your audience	

II. AUDIENCE ANALYSIS STRATEGY

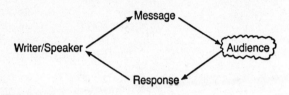

Remember that an effective communication strategy includes not only deciding what you want (determining your objective, your management style, and your credibility), but also thinking about what your audience wants. Business and professional writers and speakers often neglect their audience, with dire results: their readers or listeners may not understand them or may be needlessly offended. Analyzing your audience means determining what you know about them and how you can best motivate them.

1. What do you know about one another?

The first step in audience analysis is to consider who they are, what they know, and what you know about them. Think about the questions on the following Audience Inventory:

AUDIENCE INVENTORY

Who are they?

Primary audience: Who, exactly, is receiving your message? Visualize and name them all.

Secondary, or hidden, audience: In addition to those actually receiving your message, name anyone who will hear about, need to approve, or be affected by it.

Leader: Who is the leader or key decision-maker?

What do they know?

About you: Who are you, as far as your audience is concerned? Who or what do you represent? How much or how little do they know about you?

About your topic: What do they know about your topic? What is their attitude toward it likely to be?

About your relationship to your topic: How does your audience perceive your relation to your topic? How do they perceive your expertise or reputation?

What do you know about them?

As individuals: What is their age, sex, educational level, training, and background? What are their opinions and interests? Do they want to hear your message? What ideas are they likely to agree with? To disagree with?

As group members: What are their group characteristics? What does the group stand for? What are their shared norms, traditions, standards, rules, and values?

As they relate to you: Are they internal or external to your company or organization? If external, are they clients, customers, salespeople, colleagues, shareholders, or stakeholders? If internal, are they your superiors, subordinates, or equals? How do they perceive your rank or status?

2. How can you motivate your audience?

Once you have analyzed the members of your audience, consider what your message can do for them and how you can appeal to them most effectively.

Punish or reward them   Although threats and punishment are sometimes clearly necessary, use with caution. Remember that threats may (1) work only when you are on the spot to assure compliance; (2) eliminate undesired behavior but not necessarily produce the desired behavior; (3) produce tension, making the workplace less pleasant and productive; (4) lead people to dislike you, making it hard to enlist support or improve performance in general; and (5) provoke counteraggression.

Instead, consider using rewards as a way to change behavior. Many psychologists would argue that what they call *positive reinforcement*, or rewards, is the most effective way to motivate people.

Given the overwhelming evidence that rewards are powerful agents for influencing people, the next logical question is: How can you reward people effectively? You are likely to be successful if your rewards include four characteristics. First, they must be important to the person who is receiving them. Some people react to group acceptance, some to money, and others to recognition of achievement. Second, rewards must be appropriate (not too large, not too small) and sincere. Third, they should be immediate. The longer you wait, the less effective your rewards will be. Finally, rewards don't have to be elegant; even simple verbal recognition is an effective reward.

In general, most managers could be more successful if they used punishment less and rewards more often.

Appeal to their "growth needs" Obviously, in most situations you won't be able to reward your audience with tangible prizes. Therefore, you must search for effective intangible rewards.

One set of theories you may find helpful is Maslow's needs hierarchy and Herzberg's related research. Both researchers identified two sets of needs that motivate people: *deficiency needs* and *growth needs*. The former are needs without which we cannot survive—such as food, water, sleep, shelter. Growth needs, on the other hand, are needs that enhance our lives—such as affiliation, esteem, accomplishment, advancement.

Although deficiency needs are the most basic needs, they are not necessarily the most effective ones to appeal to. For one thing, in most managerial communication they simply do not apply. You cannot say, for example, "If you aren't persuaded by this memo or letter, I'll kill you!" In addition, Herzberg's research shows that deficiency needs are not the positive motivators that growth needs are. He cites such growth needs as pride in achievement, recognition by others, enjoyment of the work itself, and responsibility as the most important factors in persuasion.

What all this research bodes for managerial communication is this: if you want to motivate someone with rewards, consider the extraordinary persuasive power of the growth needs. For example, if you are trying to get people to work together to devise a new plan, you might appeal to their need for esteem or recognition by pointing out how much you value their suggestions; if you are writing a report, you might appeal to their need for affiliation, or relationship, by pointing out the pride they may take in the accomplishments of the division as a whole. Stress as much as possible how your message contributes to the fulfillment of your audience's growth needs

Use people's need for "balance" The use of growth needs can be even more effective if you couple them with the need for balance. According to proponents of balance theory, (1) people prefer a state of psychological balance (variously termed "consistency," "equilibrium," or "freedom from anxiety"); (2) when they hear ideas that conflict with what they already believe, they lose that state of balance and feel anxious; and (3) when they feel anxious, they attempt to restore their sense of balance.

How can you use people's need for balance to get them to accept your idea?

First, emphasize an anxiety or a problem that is causing them "imbalance," then offer a solution that will make them feel balanced. Say you are trying to persuade your boss to hold staff meetings, but he or she is dead set against them. You might emphasize the anxiety (department morale is low; turnover is high; absenteeism is increasing) and then provide balance by solving the problem (therefore, we should hold weekly staff meetings).

Second, tie the potentially unbalancing information to their needs. For example, if you are trying to persuade the budget committee to purchase new equipment for your office, and you know the basic inclination of committee members is to cut back on spending, tie your request to what is important to them: increased productivity, cost savings, perhaps even decreased time spent in their budget meetings.

Third, encourage active participation. Sometimes, if you can get people participating, they will "balance," or convince themselves they are participating in something worthwhile. (In other words, change their behavior first and their minds second.)

Fourth, concentrate on key features. If audience members are sold on two or three key features of your proposal, they will tend to sell themselves on the other features as well in order to bring their perceptions into balance. Therefore, consider choosing key points with which they will agree before you throw the whole idea at them.

Perform a cost/benefit analysis   Another way of thinking about what motivates people is to apply economic ideas to psychology.

Just like money, goods, and services, behavior can be offered for exchange. To apply this approach to communication, think of the communicator (like a seller) and the audience (like a buyer) taking into account both the cost and the benefit of the behavior. Therefore, a strong benefit will motivate your audience; a high cost will be less likely to do so. Such an approach by the communicator is essentially a cost/benefit analysis.

Using this approach, you might try three tactics to increase your persuasiveness. First, analyze both the costs and the benefits of the idea itself. Many of us tend to look only at the potential benefits, not thinking of the possible disadvantages. Perhaps you should not even send the message. Second, analyze both the costs and the benefits for your audience. Again, we frequently see just the potential rewards for ourselves and ignore the potential costs for others. Third, specify the benefits your audience will gain. Too often we assume people will see the benefits of what we are proposing when instead we should try to emphasize what's in it for them.

III. MESSAGE STRUCTURE STRATEGY

Structuring your message is the third step in setting your communication strategy. Unless you are communicating within the confines of a predetermined or standardized format, structure your message to emphasize your key ideas appropriately for your audience.

1. What do you want to emphasize?

On the basis of your communication objective, decide what you want to emphasize. Keep in mind the following graph, which shows what your audience is likely to remember:

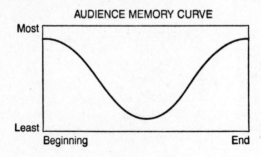

What does the audience memory curve imply? First, that you should state your important ideas prominently, either at the beginning or at the end. Second, that you should never bury important ideas in the middle. Finally, that you need to keep your audience's attention throughout by using the appeals described in the previous section.

Remembering the audience memory curve, select the most persuasive structure for presenting your message to your audience.

2. Is your audience likely to agree, interested in results, very busy?

Choose a direct strategy   When you use direct strategy, state your generalization or conclusion first, then provide specific support. For example:

The committee recommends Policy X for the following reasons:

Reason 1

Reason 2

Reason 3

The direct approach has many advantages. First, research shows that people assimilate and comprehend content more easily when they know the conclusions first. Second, the approach is audience-centered, because it emphasizes the results of your analysis—unlike the indirect approach, which is writer- or speaker-centered because it mirrors the steps you went through to formulate your conclusions. Third, the direct approach is particularly useful for memos and reports, where subject headings or recommendations sections often come first. Finally, and perhaps most importantly, the direct approach saves your audience time. Writing expert Robert Gunning sums up this argument for a direct structure: "When you read a mystery story, when you go to a movie, you hope to be entertained for an evening or for several hours. You want suspense. . . . But when you read for information, quite the opposite is true. In reading for information, one resents every moment he has to spend."

Present your views first   If you are presenting alternatives, present your views first. If your audience is likely to agree, they will be anxious to see the solution. If they are busy, they will be able to skim more quickly.

Use your strongest evidence first   For an audience that is likely to agree, interested in your conclusions, or busy, use your strongest evidence first.

3. Is your audience likely to disagree, interested in analysis?

Choose an indirect strategy   An indirect strategy involves spelling out your support first, then finishing with your generalization or conclusion. For example:

> Reason 1
> Reason 2
> Reason 3

> Therefore, the committee recommends Policy X.

The indirect approach has its own advantages. First, it may soften your audience's resistance. Second, it may arouse their interest and curiosity. Third, especially if the issues are very important or your initial credibility is relatively low, it may increase your audience's tendency to see you as fair-minded.

Present your views last   If your audience is likely to disagree, you will be more persuasive if you save your own views for the end. For one thing, presenting your views last will make your audience tend to see you as being more fair. Another advantage of presenting your views last is that you can present a series of rejected alternatives. You will be more persuasive by stating and rejecting alternatives for your audience than by having them devise their own alternatives, which they will not be as likely to reject.

Use your best evidence last   Finally, if your audience is likely to disagree, save your strongest support for the end. Use your beginning to arouse their interest and to get them to "buy in" either to ideas with which they will agree or to a problem or anxiety they need to solve.

IV. CHANNEL CHOICE STRATEGY

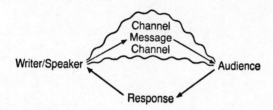

When should you write and when should you speak? If you have a choice, base your decision on your objective, your audience, and the characteristics of the three basic mediums, or channels, of communication: writing, speaking to a group, and speaking to one person. (Writing is discussed in Chapters II and III of this book, speaking in Chapters IV and V.)

Of course, communication within these channels may vary—from formal to informal, from authoritarian to participative. Nevertheless, each channel has certain inherent characteristics. The following table describes each channel in terms of time, cost, precision, place, detail, privacy, relationship, record, and response. Following the table you will find a checklist that includes a summary of the criteria for using each channel.

CHOOSING AN EFFECTIVE COMMUNICATION CHANNEL

	Writing	Speaking — To a Group	Speaking — To One Person
Time	Writer's preparation time usually high: drafting, editing	Speaker's preparation time varies: practicing, preparing, arranging	Speaker's preparation time usually low
	Reader's time usually shortest: reading takes less time than listening	Listeners' time usually longer: listening takes more time than reading	
	Writer does not control whether, when, and how thoroughly message will be read	Speaker controls when and how thoroughly message will be heard	
	Transmission time may be slower *		Transmission time may be faster
Cost	Writer's time	Speaker's time	
	Reader's time: relatively short	Listeners' time: relatively long	
	Secretarial help, materials, filing Possible postage	Possible travel and facility expenses *	Possible telephone expenses

	Readers receive exactly the same information	Listeners receive approximately the same information *	Listeners may hear differing information *
Precision			
Place	Readers need not be in same place	Listeners must be in same place *	Listener may be either face-to-face or on the telephone
Detail	May be very detailed	May be moderately detailed	Usually less detailed
Privacy	May be very private	Not private	May be very private
Relationship	May be impersonal	May build group relationships	May build individual relationships
	Less spontaneous	More spontaneous	Most spontaneous
Record	Permanent, legal record	Usually no permanent record *	Usually no permanent record *
	May be delayed	Immediate	
Response	Does not include nonverbal	Includes nonverbal	May include nonverbal
	Writers may be unaware of reader response unless they build in a response mechanism	Depending on the style of presentation, may range from limited to extensive	Usually most extensive

*Unless you use electronic mail, teleconferences, or video/audio tape recordings

CHECKLIST
COMMUNICATION STRATEGY

I. Writer/speaker strategy
   1. Your objectives:
      State your general objective(s).
      State your action objective(s): "To accomplish a specific result by a specific time."
      State your communication objective(s): "As a result of this communication, my audience will _____."
   2. Your managerial style:
      State your managerial style in terms of the Tannenbaum and Schmidt model: tell, sell, consult, or join.
   3. Your credibility:
      Analyze your initial credibility.
      Consider how to enhance or acquire credibility.

II. Audience analysis strategy
   1. Audience members:
      List the members of your primary audience.
      List the members of your secondary, or hidden, audience.
      Name the leader(s) or key decision-maker(s).
   2. Audience knowledge:
      State what your audience knows about you and what you represent to them.
      State what your audience knows about your topic and their likely attitude toward it.
      State your audience's probable perception of your relation to your topic: your expertise, reputation, and competence.
   3. Audience attitudes:
      State what you know about your audience as individuals.
      State what you know about your audience as group members.
      State what you know about your audience's attitude toward you.
   4. Audience benefits:
      State how you might punish or reward your audience.
      State how you might appeal to their growth needs.
      State how you might use their need for balance.
      Perform a cost/benefit analysis.

III. Message structure strategy
  1. Emphasis:
    Decide what points you want to emphasize and whether to place them at the beginning or at the end.
  2. Agreeable, results-oriented, or busy audiences:
    Use a direct approach.
    Present your views and your strongest evidence first.
  3. Hostile or analysis-oriented audiences:
    Use an indirect approach.
    Present your views and strongest evidence last.

IV. Channel choice strategy
When you have the choice,
  1. Write if:
    you have the time to prepare;
    your audience's time is limited;
    secretarial, material, and postage costs are not prohibitive;
    you need to communicate a great deal of detailed, precise information·
    you need a permanent, legal record;
    you do not need an immediate response; or
    you do not need a response at all (for example, if the purpose of your communication is to clarify, to confirm, to announce, or to report).
  2. Give an oral presentation if:
    you have time to prepare and arrange;
    your audience has time to attend;
    the cost of getting the group together is not prohibitive;
    you need a group of people to hear or discuss the same information at the same time;
    you want to build a group identity or relationship; or
    you want a group response, which includes a nonverbal response and may include consensus.
  3. Speak to a person individually if:
    you do not have much time to prepare;
    you need a very fast answer;
    telephone costs are not prohibitive;
    you do not need to communicate a great deal of detailed information;
    you want to build an individual relationship;
    you do not need a permanent record; or
    you need extensive, immediate feedback.

OUTLINE
WRITING: THE PROCESS

I. Compose efficiently.
    1. Generate your material.
    2. Organize your material.
    3. Draft, then edit.
    4. Avoid writer's block.

II. Select an appropriate format.
    1. Use highlighting to show structure and emphasis.
    2. Use the conventions of business formats.

II

WRITING:
THE PROCESS

Before you start to write, be sure you have established your communication strategy as described in the previous chapter: analyze your own objectives, managerial style, and credibility; consider the people in your audience and how to motivate them; structure your message appropriately for your audience; and choose the correct communication channel. Only then are you ready to start writing.

Many writers assume they can improve their writing simply by checking it for the kinds of criteria we will cover in Chapter III: cutting wordiness, inserting transitions, and so forth. This assumption is usually not true. Writers must deal with another, more pervasive, problem first—clarifying their thinking. Therefore, in this chapter we will discuss the process of writing: how to think, organize, draft, edit, and use formats efficiently. Following the steps outlined in this chapter will help you organize your thoughts, avoid writer's block, and make changes without wasting time. Don't bother with the checklist in Chapter III until you have completed these steps.

The steps for efficient composition are: (1) generating your material, (2) organizing your material, (3) drafting, then editing, and (4) avoiding writer's block. The steps for selecting an appropriate format are: (1) highlighting to show structure and emphasis; and (2) using the conventions of business formats.

I. COMPOSE EFFICIENTLY

Thinking and writing are two different processes. When you think, all kinds of ideas occur to you—some good, some bad, some complete, some fragmented. The result of the thinking process is your conclusion. When you write, on the other hand, you don't want your audience to have to wade through all the false starts and disjointed ideas you went through. Instead, you want to show them a clear, direct path to your conclusion.

The difference between thinking and writing may be illustrated as follows:

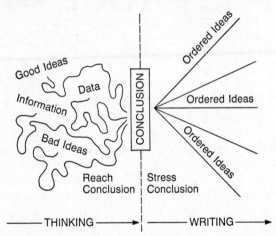

Instead of writing down ideas in the order they happen to occur to you, then, think of the writing process as four distinct steps: (1) generating your material, (2) organizing your material, (3) drafting, then editing, and (4) avoiding writer's block.

1. Generate your material

The first step in the writing process is to gather relevant data. In routine situations, where you have a simple message and easily available data, you may want to skip this step and go right to the second step, organizing your material. However, the more complex, important, and long the message, the more important this information-gathering stage becomes.

Approaches to generating information fall into three major categories: intuitive, analytic, and synthesizing.

Intuitive methods   Many writing experts discourage the use of intuitive approaches by business and professional writers. In my experience, however, many such writers, precisely because they are prone to be analytical, find intuitive approaches helpful for avoiding writer's block in the prewriting stage.

When using intuitive methods, let your mind express itself freely. Postpone analyzing and organizing until the second step in the writing process.

INTUITIVE METHODS

Brainstorming (may be done alone or with other people)

Stage 1

1. Agree on a time limit in advance.
2. Always record all ideas: write them down or tape the session.
3. Define your general topic.
4. Blurt out, jot down, or enter on a word processor every association that comes to mind, always recording.
5. Continue to associate freely and follow up on ideas; do not worry about reaching a conclusion.
6. Do not criticize any ideas.

Stage 2

7. Review the list of jottings, grouping related ideas and striking irrelevant ones.
8. Experiment with statements that express the essence of each category.

Free Writing

1. Decide on a time limit in advance.
2. Keep your pen or pencil moving, or keep typing.
3. If you cannot think of anything to say, write "nothing to say" over and over until you do think of something.
4. Be as spontaneous as possible; don't edit; don't analyze.

Journal or Notes

1. Keep a journal or notebook with you over a period of time.
2. As ideas occur to you (in the car, in bed, after you shower), jot them down.

Analytic methods   Analytic methods are generally more orderly and quick than intuitive approaches. They may, however, produce more mechanical or less original results.

ANALYTIC METHODS

Focusing

1. Define your general topic.
2. Focus on one aspect of your topic.
3. Break this aspect into more specific subtopics.
4. Focus on the second aspect of your topic.
5. Break the second aspect into more specific subtopics.
6. Continue in this way for each aspect of your topic.

Journalists' questioning

Answer the journalists' set of questions·

1. Who?
2. What?
3. Where?
4. When?
5. How?
6. Why?

Rhetorical questioning

Answer any of these rhetorical questions that apply:

1. What does X mean?
2. How can X be described?
3. What are the component parts of X?
4. How is X made or done?
5. How should X be made or done?
6. What are the causes of X?
7. What are the consequences of X?
8. How does X compare with Y?

Synthesizing methods   These methods are often used in business and professional prewriting. They rely on encountering and adapting new ideas to generate information.

SYNTHESIZING METHODS

Reading

1. Read flexibly: skim irrelevant sections; slow down for important sections.
2. Read actively, scribbling in the margins, underlining, and taking notes.
3. Beware of plagiarism; always acknowledge your sources.

Interviewing

1. Use good body language: appropriate eye contact; open, relaxed posture; energy in your voice, gestures, and facial expression.
2. Use encouragements to talk: nonverbal, such as nodding; verbal, such as "I see" or "uh-huh."
3. To generate the most information, ask open-ended questions—those that cannot be answered "Yes" or "No."
4. Paraphrase or summarize to show you are listening, to make sure you have understood, and to elicit further information.
5. Ask for details, examples, or clarification to encourage more specific information.*

*See Chapter IV, Section 3, for more information on effective listening.

---

2. Organize your material

After you have used these prewriting methods to generate information, the second step is to organize that information for your reader. In the words of one expert, *Harvard Business Review* editor David Ewing, "one of the most common misconceptions is that the reader wants a blow-by-blow account of how the writer came to his or her conclusions. When you make this error, . . . you lead off with what you saw and heard in the first phase, and then you describe what the next series of tests or interviews produced, then you give the highlights of what you learned in the next phase, and sooner or later you come to your conclusions or recommendations."

Instead of merely mirroring your thought process, organize clearly by (1) providing a hierarchy for your ideas, and (2) putting your ideas in order.

Provide a hierarchy for your ideas   Effective organization is based on providing a hierarchy of ideas for your audience. In other words, you divide ideas into groups and differentiate among those groups. To provide a clear hierarchy, you stress your conclusion (or first-level idea), divide your message into main points (or second-level ideas), and subdivide these into supporting points.

1. Stress your conclusion (first-level idea)   Your conclusion, of course, is the most important idea in your communication. It's the result of all your time and analysis; it's closely tied to your communication objective ("As a result of this message, my audience will _____.") Sample conclusions might be:

> Steps in a procedure I want them to follow
>
> Reasons why they should buy this product
>
> Recommendations I want them to approve

In stressing your conclusion, keep in mind the audience memory curve illustrated in Chapter I: your audience is likely to recall what you state at the beginning and at the end. Therefore, place your conclusion prominently—at the beginning or end, not buried in the middle.

2. Divide into second-level points Your second-level points are the main divisions into which you divide your writing, such as:

Four steps in the procedure

Five reasons why they should buy this product

Three recommendations for approval

To ascertain your second-level ideas, again in the words of David Ewing, "you need to do the same thing that practically every good writer has done since the first cogent stone tablet was written by a caveperson: Step back mentally from the details and try to see the essence of the message." Specifically, Ewing suggests three possible methods. First, imagine you meet your reader or listener on the street. He or she is in a great hurry, so you must explain your ideas within two minutes. What would you say? Second, imagine you had to send a telegram to your reader or listener, paying some outrageous price per word. How would you encapsulate your main ideas to save money? Finally, try asking yourself, "What do my readers need to know most? If they only skim my writing, what is the absolute minimum they should learn?"

Another writing expert, Linda Flower, refers to this process of dividing into second-level ideas as "nutshelling and teaching your main ideas." She suggests: "In two or three sentences—in a nutshell—try to lay out the whole substance of your paper. Nutshelling practically forces you to distinguish major ideas from minor ones and to decide how those major ideas are related to one another. . . . Once you can express your idea in a nutshell to yourself, think about how you would *teach* those ideas to someone else. . . . Like nutshelling, trying to teach your ideas helps you form concepts so that your listener gets *the point*, not just a list of facts."

3. Subdivide into lower-level points   Your second-level ideas are in turn supported by your lower-level points. Most experts today agree that idea charts are more effective than traditional outlines for subdividing your ideas. Idea charts look like pyramids or upside-down trees; therefore, they have been termed *idea trees* or what writing expert Barbara Minto calls *idea pyramids*.

When you put together an idea chart, you can list your ideas informally. You can group your ideas by similar subject matter: "This is problem X; that is problem Y"; "This is reason X; that is reason Y"; "This is recommendation X; that is recommendation Y." Then, you can develop key overarching concepts that summarize and label each grouping: "What I have here is a series of problems (reasons, recommendations)."

Idea charts offer you at least three advantages over traditional outlines. First, they let you see the whole picture and how parts fit: they are more visual than an outline. They also allow you to change, add to, or omit information that does not fit: they are more flexible than an outline. Finally, they can actually help you come up with ideas.

As you sketch an idea chart, keep in mind three rules of thumb. First, make sure any higher-level idea generalizes or summarizes about all the lower-level ideas branching out below it. Second, check that all branches at the same level are the same kind of idea—for example, all reasons, all steps, all problems, or all recommendations. Last, limit the number of branches on your upside-down tree. Your audience's short-term working memory, its attention span, can handle only five to seven main points. This means you should group no more than five to seven main branches on any level.

EXAMPLE: PROVIDING A HIERARCHY

No hierarchy

Eliminate product X.
Provide *pro forma* financial statements.
Define responsibilities within departments.
Do not approach shareholders for more capital.
Expand marketing division.
Concentrate on product Y.
Renegotiate short-term liability with banks.

Clear hierarchy

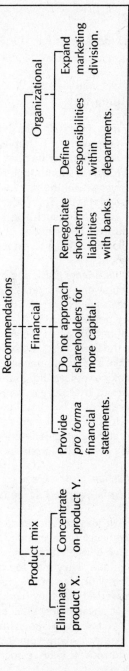

Put your ideas in order   Once you have put together your hierarchy of ideas, you need to decide the order in which to present them.

1. For explanatory ideas   Place your first-level idea first. Then, order in one of three ways.

   a. *By time.* This is an effective order for historical background or for steps in a process. For example, if you were explaining a payroll procedure, you would order by time: (1) submit withdrawal forms a month before payday; (2) submit time reports two weeks before payday; (3) pick up paychecks on the first of the month.
   b. *By components.* This order is most useful if you are describing existing classifications, such as geographical or spatial divisions. For example, if you were reporting on profit analysis for divisions, you might order as follows: (1) West Coast region, (2) Midwest region, and (3) East Coast region.
   c. *By importance.* Ordering by importance is more difficult than ordering by time or components. When you order by time, most people agree on the sequence. When you order by components, you are not implying any priorities (in the case of a regional division from west to east, you're not implying that the West Coast is more important than the Midwest or the East Coast). When you order by importance, however, you must make a value judgment. Here you want to show priorities; you want to rank your ideas. For example, you might analyze the problems in your current inventory system like this: (1) most important problem, (2) second most important problem, (3) third most important problem, and so forth. Since you are making judgments, be sure to use the communication strategies described in Chapter I to analyze how your audience will assess the importance of these ideas.

2. For action ideas   Order your ideas on the basis of whether your audience is likely to agree or disagree.

   a. *Likely to agree.* Your audience might be likely to agree for many reasons. Audience members may be busy with many other projects. They may have delegated the question to you or asked you to come up with a solution. They may see you as an expert in this particular area, someone with high initial credibility. Finally, the topic may be so uncontroversial that they have no strong opinions one way or the other.
   In these cases, your audience will want to see your ideas clearly. Therefore, you should use the direct approach, as we discussed in Chapter I—with your top-level idea first, where they can see it easily, and your strongest evidence first, where they will be more likely to hear or read it.

b. *Likely to disagree.* Your audience may be hostile or threatened. Your topic might be so controversial or delicate that they feel anxious. They may see you as someone with very low initial credibility.

In these cases, use the indirect approach, as we discussed in Chapter I: state your least controversial points first; present rejected alternatives before your own recommendation; and use your strongest evidence last.

EXAMPLE: ORDERING IDEAS

Case 1

Your busy boss has delegated a decision to you and wants a clear-cut solution. In this case, you might state your recommendation first and clearly, then present your strongest evidence at once:

> I recommend that we cut back on the widget line. The main reason for this recommendation is that widgets lack the potential for long-term growth. (followed by your analysis)

Case 2

Your boss is concerned about the widget line. She has been personally involved with its current success. She is also concerned with the future of the company, of course, and has asked for your tentative opinion. In this case, you might open with an idea with which you know she will agree ("We don't want to sacrifice our future profits. . . ."). The rejected negative argument ("Although widgets contribute enormously to our current profits, . . .")—which is also tied to her pride and achievement in the current line—might precede your recommendation and strongest point, which appear at the end:

> We don't want to sacrifice our future profits for the sake of short-term gains. Therefore, although widgets contribute enormously to our current profits, we must consider cutting back on that line because of its lack of long-term growth potential. (followed by your analysis)

---

3. Draft, then edit

After you have organized your thoughts into a visual outline or idea chart, you are ready to start writing. Remember that if you start writing without an organizational blueprint, you risk wasting your time and lessening your reader's comprehension.

Drafting and editing are two very different kinds of processes. Avoid writer's block and save time by separating these two stages.

Drafting Your attitude is crucial during the draft stage. Don't allow yourself to be a perfectionist. Think of drafting as creative, editing as analytical; do not edit as you draft. Here are some techniques to help you in the drafting stage.

1. *Avoid editing* Do not worry about specific problems as you write your draft. Do not edit. If you cannot think of a word, leave a blank space; if you cannot decide between two words, write them both down. Circle or put a check mark in the margin next to awkward or unclear sections, and come back to them later.

2. *Get a typed copy* As you draft, avoiding detailed editing, somehow get a typed copy—one side only, double- or triple-spaced, with wide margins. You will save time if you avoid handwriting: you write in longhand at about 15 words per minute; you can type at 20 to 60 words per minute; you can dictate at 65 to 95 words per minute. Furthermore, you will find it much easier to spot and correct errors if you can edit from a typed copy. To get your typed copy, you may type on a standard typewriter; keyboard onto a word processor; or dictate to a person, a machine, or a telephone hookup.

3. *Don't force beginning-to-end composition* Regardless of how you choose to get your draft into typed copy, you do not necessarily have to write from beginning to end. Many writers get bogged down in their introduction or first section. Besides, writers often have to change their introduction because they have modified their ideas or organizations when composing the rest of the draft. Writing your introduction last may help you avoid both of these problems. Consider writing first the sections you are most comfortable with.

4. Schedule a time gap   You are guaranteed a better job of editing if you leave some time between the drafting and editing stages. For important or complex documents, separate the two stages by an overnight break. If you are under severe time constraints, or if you are composing a routine communication, leave yourself a shorter gap: for example, begin editing after lunch or even a five-to-ten-minute break.

Editing   When you begin editing, don't immediately agonize over commas and word choice. Instead, complete the four-step plan that follows. It will save you time by allowing you to cut or modify sections before you have wasted time perfecting them.

1. Edit for communication strategy   Before you begin fine-tuning, make sure you have written according to your communication strategy. Ask yourself these questions: Have you accomplished your objective, and is it written in the appropriate style, given your credibility? Have you written at the appropriate intellectual and emotional levels for your audience? Have you motivated your audience? Have you emphasized your main idea(s)? Is your structure appropriate for your audience? Should this message be in written form at all? (See Chapter I for elaboration of all of these communication-strategy issues.)

2. Edit for organization   Second, make sure your writing is well organized. Have you provided a clear hierarchy of ideas? Can the reader see the difference among your top-level, second-level, and lower-level points? Have you ordered your ideas appropriately (explanatory ideas by time, components, or importance; action ideas based on your audience's likelihood to agree or disagree)? Is your format consistent, concise, and parallel? Have you used the conventional business formats? (This chapter covers these ideas.)

3. Edit for good writing   Once you have edited for strategy and organization, edit for good writing— as we shall discuss in the next chapter. Check your document and paragraphs. Check your sentences and words. (See Chapter III for an explanation of the principles of good writing.)

4. Check your grammar and punctuation.   If you have any questions on grammar and punctuation, refer to Chapter VI.

4. Avoid writer's block

If you use these techniques for drafting and editing, you should be able to alleviate problems with writer's block. Writing is difficult work. No formula, alas, will free you from that work. However, there are some ways to avoid the most common pitfalls in the writing process.

1. *Expect complexity*   Remember that writing is not merely a matter of inspiration that comes easily to everyone else. It is a complex process involving various stages, not a simple one-step magic formula.

2. *Schedule your time*   You don't have to finish in one session. Separate your prewriting, drafting, and editing stages. Allow several days or at least overnight for important and complicated documents; allow an hour, a lunch break, or a coffee break for less important or routine documents.

3. *Differentiate thinking from organizing*   Clear thinking and clear writing are related, but they are not identical. Order your ideas appropriately for your reader; don't just write in the order that the ideas occurred to you.

4. *Organize before you write*   Never start to write without an idea chart. Order your ideas before you start to put them into paragraph and sentence form. You may change your organization as you write, but you will waste time if you start writing with no plan or direction.

5. *Separate drafting from editing*   Do not try to edit during the drafting stage; instead, just let your creativity flow. Do not worry about specifics; you can come back and fix them later. You do not have to write straight through from beginning to end. Do not try to "finish one thing at a time"; you can revise later.

6. *Try techniques for editing*   If you bog down during the editing stage, try imagining you are talking to your reader, free-writing for a while, or talking into a tape recorder.

7. Edit from a typed copy   Edit a typed copy, whether from a typewriter, word processor, or dictation. Use one side only, double- or triple-spaced. Typed copies are much easier to correct.

8. Move sections around if necessary   Do not waste time rewriting or retyping sections that do not need to be changed. Instead, move sections—by machine if you're using a word processor, with scissors and tape if you're using paper.

9. Expect to rethink   Although organizing, drafting, and editing are different stages in the writing process, don't expect them to be completely distinct from one another; don't expect to march in lockstep logically and smoothly from one stage to the next. Instead, during any one of these stages, expect the writing process to be what the experts call "recursive," that is, expect to rethink, to go back, to make changes. For example, as you write your draft, you may discover and fix flaws in your organization. As you do your final editing, you may discover and fix problems with your overall strategy. If you expect this kind of continual rethinking, you will avoid bogging down when the need for it occurs.

II. SELECT AN APPROPRIATE FORMAT

A second set of decisions involved in the writing process has to do with selecting an appropriate format. One of the biggest differences between business/professional writing and other kinds is the use of format. Clear, consistent formats are a great boon to business and professional readers—that is, readers with limited time. Since your readers are busy, make your ideas "visually apparent"—that is, design your document so that it shows your organization.

Preparing a format should include: (1) highlighting your structure and main ideas, and (2) using conventional business forms (memos, reports, and letters).

1. Use highlighting to show structure and emphasis

Highlighting—the use of headings, subheadings, indentations, bullet points, or lists—is appropriate in almost every business communication. In general, your message has a better chance of being read, remembered, and acted upon if you highlight.

Highlighting benefits your readers in two ways. First, it shows your organization. These two examples signal your reader that a list of recommendations and steps in a procedure will follow:

Recommendations: role of the CEO

Procedure for new inventory system

Second, highlighting can emphasize your main ideas. For example, here are two main ideas that might follow under recommendations for the role of the CEO:

Develop long-term strategy.

Provide legal counsel.

Rules for highlighting   Whether you are using highlighting to show your structure or your main ideas, keep in mind these four rules.

1. Be consistent   Always indent consistently. For example, indent all your paragraphs throughout, or use unindented paragraphs throughout. Always label consistently, using numbers, letters, bullet points, or decimals in the same manner throughout. Finally, use the same typography for the same level of ideas throughout.

> *Poor:*   MINUTES OF MARCH 28 MEETING (main heading)
> PROGRESS REPORT FROM THE ABC DIVISION (secondary heading)
> Progress report from the XYZ Division (secondary heading)
>
> *Improved:*   MINUTES OF MARCH 28 MEETING
> Progress report from the ABC Division
> Progress report from the XYZ Division

2. Prefer idea headings to category headings   Idea headings are "stand-alone" headings that capture the essence of your ideas—headings a reader can skim and understand without referring to the rest of the text. Your reader could skim *category headings*, on the other hand, and have no idea what you are writing about.

> *Category headings:*   BENEFITS
> BACKGROUND
> RESULTS
>
> *Idea headings:*   BENEFITS OF X PRODUCT
> 1. You will save time.
>   (followed by section on time savings)
> 2. You will save money.
>   (followed by section on money savings)

3. Don't overdo highlighting   Limit the amount of material you highlight; limit the wording of the sentences and phrases you highlight.

> *Poor:*   In order to grow, we should consider decentralizing for the following reasons:
>
> *Improved:*   Benefits of decentralizing

> *Poor:*   To increase production of X to establish market position, I submit that we continue to buy (rather than start to produce) component Y.
>
> *Improved:*   Continue to buy component Y.

4. Use parallelism: show equally important ideas in the same grammatical form   Use the same grammatical form for the wording of each heading or subheading. The first word could be an active verb, a verb with an *-ing* ending, or a noun—but you must be consistent in your choice.

> *Poor:*   Steps to organize internally:
>   1. Establishing formal sales organization.
>   2. Definition of responsibilities with the production department.
>   3. Improve cost-accounting system.
>
> *Improved:*   Steps to organize internally:
>   1. Establish formal sales organization.
>   2. Define responsibilities within the production department.
>   3. Improve cost-accounting system.

Layouts for highlighting Keeping in mind these four rules for high-lighting choose from the various layouts for highlighting—which include any consistent mixture of headings, subheadings, indentations, bullet points, lists, and labels. Any of the following examples, any combination of them, or any method your organization prescribes will be effective as long as you use the same method consistently.

The following five layouts are among the most frequently used:

OUTLINE LAYOUT

Place increasingly subordinate ideas ever further to the right of the page, and label (number and letter) as in a formal outline.

I. TITLE HEADING I
IIIIIIIIIIIIIIIIIIIIIIIIIIIIIIIIIIIIIIIIIIIIIIIIIIIIIIIIIIIIIIIIIIIIIIIIIIIIIIIIIIIIIIIIIIIIIIIIIIIIIIIIIIIIIIIIIII
IIIIIIIIIIIIIIIIIIIIIIIIIIIIIIIIIIIIIIIIIIIIIIIIIIIIIIIIIIIIIIIIIIIII

A. PRIMARY SECTION HEADING A

  AAAAAAAAAAAAAAAAAAAAAAAAAAAAAAAAAAAAAAAAAAAAAAAAAAAA
  AAAAAAAAAAAAAAAAAAAAAAAAAAAAAAA

  1. Secondary Heading 1

    1111111111111111111111111111111111111111111111111111111
    11111111111111111111111111111111111

    a. Tertiary heading a

      aaaaaaaaaaaaaaaaaaaaaaaaaaaaaaaaaaaaaaaaaaaaaaaaaaaaaaaaaaaa
      aaaaaaaaaaaaaaaaaaaaaaaaaaaaaaaaaaaaaaaaaaaaaaa

MODIFIED OUTLINE LAYOUT

Use typography (capital letters, lowercase letters, underlines, italics) rather than the labels (numbers and letters) of a more formal outline.

TITLE HEADING I

PRIMARY SECTION HEADING A
AAAAAAAAAAAAAAAAAAAAAAAAAAAAAAAAAAAAAAAAAAAAAAAAAAAAA
AAAAAAAAAAAAAAAAAAAAAAAAAAAAAAAAAA
Secondary Heading 1
11111111111111111111111111111111111111111111111111111111
11111111111111111111111111111111111
Tertiary heading a
aaaaaaaaaaaaaaaaaaaaaaaaaaaaaaaaaaaaaaaaaaaaaaaaaaaaaaaaaaaaaa
aaaaaaaaaaaaaaaaaaaaaaaaaaaaaaaaaaaaa

BULLET LAYOUT

Use bullet points (•) or dashes (—) instead of the numbers and letters of a more formal outline.

TITLE HEADING I

PRIMARY SECTION HEADING A

AAAAAAAAAAAAAAAAAAAAAAAAAAAAAAAAAAAAAAAAAAAAAAAAAAAAA
AAAAAAAAAAAAAAAAAAAAAA

• Secondary Heading 1

11111111111111111111111111111111111111111111111111111111
11111111111111111111111111111111111

—Tertiary heading a: aaaaaaaaaaaaaaaaaaaaaaaaaaaaaaaaaaaaaaaaaaaaaaaa
aaaaaaaaaaaaaaaaaaaaaaaaaaaaaaaaaaaaaaaaaaaaaa

• Secondary Heading 2

222222222222222222222222222222222222222222222222222222222
2222222222222222222222222

DECIMAL LAYOUT

Place increasingly subordinate ideas ever further to the right and label with decimals. Useful for scientific and government reports.

1. TITLE HEADING I
I.1 <u>PRIMARY SECTION HEADING A</u>
AAAAAAAAAAAAAAAAAAAAAAAAAAAAAAAAAAAAAAAAAAAAAAAAAA
AAAAAAAA
  I.1.1. <u>Secondary Heading 1</u>
    1111111111111111111111111111111111111111111111111
    1111111111111111111
    I.1.1.1. <u>Tertiary heading a</u>
      aaaaaaaaaaaaaaaaaaaaaaaaaaaaaaaaaaaaaaaaaaaaaa
      aaaaaaaaaaaaaaaaaaaa

INFORMAL INDENTED LAYOUT

Indent groups of similar ideas. Underline topic sentences as headings (labeled "Items" below). Useful for short memos or letters.

<u>TITLE HEADING I</u>

IIIIIIIIIIIIIIIIIIIIIIIIIIIIIIIIIIIIIIIIIIIIIIIIIIIIIIIIIIIIIIIIIIIIIIIIIIIIIIIIIIIIIIIIIIIIIIIIIIIIIIIIIIIIIIIIIIIIII
IIIIIIIIIIIIIIIIIIIIIIIIIIIIIIIIIIIIIIIIIIIIIIIIIIIIIIIIIIIIIIIIIIIIIIIIIIIIIIIIIIIII

1. <u>Item 1:</u> 11111111111111111111111111111111111111111111111
   11111111111111111111111111111111

2. <u>Item 2:</u> 2222222222222222222222222222222222222222222222222
   22222222222222222222222222222222

3. <u>Item 3:</u> 3333333333333333333333333333333333333333333333333
   33333333333333333333333333333333

2. Use the conventions of business formats

In addition to highlighting your structure and your main ideas, your format should follow the conventions of the three basic business documents: (1) letters, (2) reports or proposals, and (3) memos.

Letters   Letters are the major form of external communication.

STANDARD ELEMENTS OF A LETTER

1. Heading: Sender's address, followed by date; either on printed letterhead or typed out.

2. Inside address: Receiver's name, title, and address.

> Ms. Helen Pellegrin, Director
> Personnel Department
> XYZ Corporation
> Street Address
> City, State (two-letter abbreviation), Zip Code

3. Salutation: *Formal:*   Dear (or My dear) Ms. D'Aunno:
  Semiformal: Dear Mr. Leavitt:
  Informal: Dear Richard,

4. Closing and signature: *Formal:*   Very truly (or Sincerely) yours,
  XYZ CORPORATION

Hector Guerrero

Hector Guerrero
Director of Marketing

  Semiformal: Yours truly (or Sincerely yours),

Marilyn Wyatt

Marilyn Wyatt
Senior Consultant

  Informal: Cordially,

Lindsay

Lindsay Rahmun
Managing Partner

FULL BLOCK–LETTER FORMAT

All lines flush with left margin.

Date

Name
Address
Address

Salutation:

xxxxxxxxxxxxxxxxxxxxxxxxxxxxxxxxxxxxxxxxxxxxxxxxxxxxxxxxxxxxxxxxx
xxxxxxxxxxxxxxxxxxxxxxxxxxxxxxxxxxxxxxxxxxxxxxxxxxxxxxxxxxxxx.

xxxxxxxxxxxxxxxxxxxxxxxxxxxxxxxxxxxxxxxxxxxxxxxxxxxxxxxxxxxxxxxxx
xxxxxxxxxxxxxxxxxxxxxxxxxxxxxxxxxxxxxxxxxxxxxxxxxxxxxxxxxxxx.

Closing,

Signature

MODIFIED BLOCK–LETTER FORMAT

All lines flush with left margin except date, closing, and signature. They all start at the center of the page.

Date

Name
Address
Address

Salutation:

xxxxxxxxxxxxxxxxxxxxxxxxxxxxxxxxxxxxxxxxxxxxxxxxxxxxxxxxxxxxxxxxxxxxx
xxxxxxxxxxxxxxxxxxxxxxxxxxxxxxxxxxxxxxxxxxxxxxxxxxxxxxxxxxxxxxxxx.

xxxxxxxxxxxxxxxxxxxxxxxxxxxxxxxxxxxxxxxxxxxxxxxxxxxxxxxxxxxxxxxxxxxxx
xxxxxxxxxxxxxxxxxxxxxxxxxxxxxxxxxxxxxxxxxxxxxxxxxxxxxxxxxxxxxxxxxx.

Closing,

Signature

SEMI-BLOCK–LETTER FORMAT

Date, closing, and signature start at the center of the page. Paragraphs are indented five spaces.

                              Date

Name
Address
Address

Salutation:

     xxxxxxxxxxxxxxxxxxxxxxxxxxxxxxxxxxxxxxxxxxxxxxxxxxxxxxxxxxxxxx
xxxxxxxxxxxxxxxxxxxxxxxxxxxxxxxxxxxxxxxxxxxxxxxxxxxxxxxxxx.

     xxxxxxxxxxxxxxxxxxxxxxxxxxxxxxxxxxxxxxxxxxxxxxxxxxxxxxxxxxxxxx
xxxxxxxxxxxxxxxxxxxxxxxxxxxxxxxxxxxxxxxxxxxxxxxxxxxxxxxxxx.

                              Closing,

                              Signature

Reports or proposals   Reports and proposals, of course, may be either
internal or external.

STANDARD ELEMENTS OF A REPORT OR PROPOSAL

Preliminary information

1. Title page: Title (four-to-eight word one-phrase summary).
Receiver's name and position.
Sender's name and position.
Date.

2. Cover letter (if external)   Authorization or occasion.
   or   Scope.
Cover memo (if internal):   Acknowledgments.
Polite closing: hope to satisfy, willing to
discuss.

3. Abstract or   No more than 5 percent of total report
"executive summary":   length.
Summarize content, not just organization.

4. Table of contents: Preliminary information:
Number with small romans (i, ii, iii).
Body of report:
List all main and secondary sections.
Number with arabics (1, 2, 3).
Appendixes:
Usually lettered (Appendix A, Appendix B).
Exhibits:
Usually numbered (Exhibit I, Exhibit II).
List of illustrations or internal exhibits (optional).

5. Introduction: Not a synopsis (synopsis is included in the abstract).
Build reader interest and receptivity; explain the
reasons for writing; point your reader toward your
conclusion and organization. (See p. 56 for more
information on how to write an introduction.)

6. Conclusions (if analysis) or recommendations (if action plan)

Body of report

7. Detailed development and support: Description, explanations, evaluations, analysis.
Group and order ideas clearly.
Use headings and subheadings.

Supplementary information

8. Appendixes: Stand-alone documents: tables of data, samples of forms, copies of questionnaires, detailed descriptions of methodology, explanatory articles, *pro forma* statements, and so forth.

9. Exhibits: Charts and graphs.
(See Chapter IV, Section 3, for more information on composing exhibits.)

In addition to using the standard formats for reports, keep in mind the following characteristics of report readers. Research indicates, first, that managers tend to read only the preliminary sections of your report, especially: (1) the abstract or executive summary; (2) the introduction; and (3) the conclusions or recommendations. Fewer than half of them will be likely to read the body of your report. On the other hand, technical personnel are likely to read the body. Finally, readers are unlikely to look at the appendixes and exhibits at the back of the report. If you feel the information in an exhibit is essential, incorporate it in the body.

Memos   Memos are the major form of internal communication.

STANDARD ELEMENTS OF A MEMO

1. **Date**

2. **"To" heading:**   Receiver's name or distribution list.

3. **"From" heading:**   Sender's name.

4. **"Subject" heading:**   Make sure it is neither too broad nor too specific.

5. **Signature:**   Informal—Sign your first name next to the "From" heading.
   Semiformal—Sign your initials next to the "From" heading.
   Formal—Add salutation at the beginning and your signature at the end, in addition to the "To" and "From" headings.

FORMATS FOR MEMO HEADINGS

Most organizations provide forms with headings. Here are three typical formats:

Date:

To:
From:
Subject:

Subject·   Date:
To: From:

Date:
Subject:
To:
From:

CHECKLIST
WRITING: THE PROCESS

I. Compose efficiently.
   1. Have you generated sufficient material, using, if necessary, intuitive, analytic, or synthesizing methods?
   2. Have you organized your material clearly?
        Provide a hierarchy for your ideas: stress your conclusion or first-level idea, divide into second-level points, and subdivide into lower-level points.
        Put your ideas in order: order explanatory ideas by time, components, or importance; order action ideas based on your audience's likelihood to agree or disagree.
   3. Have you separated drafting from editing?
        In drafting avoid editing, get a typed copy, do not force beginning-to-end composition, and schedule a time gap.
        In editing, check your communication strategy (Chapter I), organization (Chapter II), general writing (Chapter III), and grammar and punctuation (Chapter VI).
   4. Have you avoided writer's block?
II. Select an appropriate format.
   1. Have you used highlighting to show your structure and emphasize important ideas?
        Check layout for consistency, concise wording, judicious use of highlighting, and parallelism.
   2. Have you used the conventions of business formats?
        Check letters, reports, and memos for correct use of standard elements.

OUTLINE
WRITING: THE PRODUCT

I Effective documents and paragraphs
1. Organization
2. Unity and emphasis
3. Coherence
4. Appropriate length

II. Effective sentences and words
1. Brevity
2. Vigor
3. Appropriate length
4. Simplicity

III

WRITING:
THE PRODUCT

Chapters I and II have discussed the writing process: strategic concerns (such as your objective, audience, and structure) and organizational concerns (such as providing a hierarchy, putting your ideas in order, and selecting a format). This chapter discusses what to look for in the final product.

The chapter consists of two major sections. The first discusses the qualities of both a well-written document and a well-written paragraph. The second section discusses the closely related issues of clear sentences and words.

I. EFFECTIVE DOCUMENTS AND PARAGRAPHS

The same four qualities characterize a well-written document and a well-written paragraph. This section defines and explains these characteristics: (1) organization, (2) unity/emphasis, (3) coherence, and (4) appropriate length.

1. Organization

The first characteristic of good document and paragraph writing is clear organization.

The document   If you have followed the process outlined in the previous chapter, your document should be well organized, because you have provided a hierarchy of ideas and ordered your ideas. If you have used the highlighting techniques outlined in the previous chapter, your clear organization will be visually apparent to your reader.

Each paragraph   Apply the same kinds of organizational criteria to each paragraph.

First, provide a hierarchy of ideas by grouping each paragraph around only one top-level idea. Each paragraph should begin with a generalization: for a standard paragraph, the generalization takes the form of a topic sentence; for a highlighted subsection, the generalization takes the form of a subheading. Each topic sentence or subheading should state clearly the leading idea, showing the reader what that paragraph or section is about.

Second, order your ideas clearly within each paragraph. The box on the next page shows the most common patterns for ordering paragraphs, each pattern followed by a sample topic sentence and a sample subheading.

PATTERNS FOR ORDERING PARAGRAPHS

Pattern	Sample topic sentence	Sample subheading
Definition	The logical way to begin is to describe product X.	Description of Product X
Classification	XYZ Corporation consists of five functional divisions.	XYZ's Organization
Comparison/ contrast	Division A and Division B differ in several major ways.	Differences: Division A and Division B
Example	The new brochures are full of major printing errors.	Printing Errors in Brochure
Process analysis	Procedure X works in a series of four steps.	Steps in Procedure X
Cause and effect	Three causes contributed to the problem at plant X.	Causes of Plant X Problems

2. Unity and emphasis

Two related qualities of good writing are unity and emphasis. Unity means avoiding extraneous material; emphasis means placing your main ideas prominently.

The document   To achieve good unity, recall your main ideas—those that accomplish your communication objective. Then, cut out any material that does not relate directly to those ideas.

To achieve good emphasis, place your main ideas at the beginning or the end of the document.

Introductions   Your introduction should accomplish three aims. First, it should build reader interest and receptivity. Most writers accomplish this by referring to an existing situation or to ideas the reader shares with them: "We need to increase our market share," "XYZ is a growing firm," or "As we discussed last Thursday," for instance. Second, your introduction should explain the changes, issues, or reasons for your writing. For example, "We have discussed possible methods with our staff," "Several problems have arisen," or "Someone suggested we do X." Finally, the introduction should point your reader toward your conclusion and organization. If you are using the direct approach, state your solutions in the same order you use in the body of the document. If you are using the indirect approach, open with a question or list of options; again, use the same order for the options in the body of the document.

Although an effective introduction includes each of these elements, you may present them in any order, depending on your credibility and your audience's needs—both of which we discussed in Chapter I. If you have high credibility or your audience wants to see your solution quickly, state your organization first. If your audience is more interested in the project itself, begin by stating the issues or changes necessitating your writing. If you have lower credibility or are less sure of your audience's agreement, build reader interest and receptivity first.

How long should an introduction be? At the most, write three paragraphs—one for each of the three aims. At the least, open with one sentence that accomplishes all three aims, such as: "As you requested last Tuesday, I have summarized my objections to the new marketing plan."

Conclusions The end of your document—your conclusion—is the other place to emphasize your main points. Avoid restating your main idea in pompous words: "Thus it becomes readily apparent that due to the fact that we have. . . ." Avoid introducing a completely new topic; this not only diverts your reader's attention from your communication objective, but it spoils your document's unity. Finally, avoid apologizing or undercutting your argument at the end.

Instead, you may choose one of three endings. First, if you are using the direct approach and if the document is long, restate your main ideas. Obviously, you don't need to reiterate three points in a one-page memo or letter. Second, if you are using the indirect approach, state your conclusions or recommendations. Third, state an *action step* or *feedback mechanism*. A typical action step might be: "I'll call you next Thursday to discuss this matter," "Please let me know if I can be of further help," or "Once I have your approval, I'll go ahead with this plan."

Each paragraph To achieve good unity, state your main idea, or generalization, in a topic sentence or subheading. Omit any sentence in the body of the paragraph that does not amplify that main idea.

To achieve good emphasis in virtually all business and professional writing, place your topic sentence or subheading at the beginning of each paragraph or section. The inverted pyramid is a useful way to visualize the structure of each paragraph:

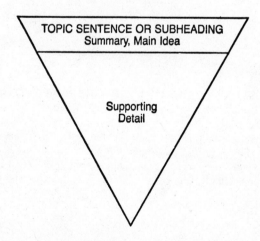

3. Coherence

Organization, unity, and emphasis are not enough to make your writing effective. Your organized, related ideas must cohere. Bridge your ideas clearly, both between and within your paragraphs, by using (1) transitions, (2) highlighting, or (3) identity signals.

Transitions   Perhaps the most familiar way to achieve coherence is to use transitional words or phrases. This list includes some of the most frequent transitions in writing:

<table>
<tr><td colspan="2" align="center">FREQUENTLY USED TRANSITIONS</td></tr>
<tr><td>To signal</td><td>Sample transitions</td></tr>
<tr><td>Addition or amplification</td><td>and, furthermore, besides, next, moreover, in addition, again, also, similarly, too, finally, second, subsequently, last</td></tr>
<tr><td>Contrast</td><td>but, or, nor, yet, still, however, nevertheless, on the contrary, on the other hand, conversely, although</td></tr>
<tr><td>Example or sequence</td><td>for example, for instance, thus, that is, first, second, third</td></tr>
<tr><td>Conclusion</td><td>therefore, thus, then, in conclusion, consequently, as a result, accordingly, finally</td></tr>
<tr><td>Time or place</td><td>at the same time, simultaneously, above, below, further on, so far, until now</td></tr>
</table>

For example, here is an executive summary from a report, with the transitions in boldface:

> XYZ Company should follow these recommendations to clear up its financial crisis. **First,** cut back drastically on labor, outside services, and manufacturing overhead expenses. **Second,** do not approach shareholders for more capital. **Finally,** renegotiate short-term liabilities with the banks.

Highlighting   A second coherence technique is to use the page layout to indicate the relationships between ideas: headings and subheadings, enumeration, bullet points and dashes, and indentations. (See Chapter II for further details on highlighting.) The following example shows how the previous executive summary could have been highlighted to allow readers to see the relations between the ideas:

OVERVIEW OF RECOMMENDATIONS
TO CLEAR UP FINANCIAL CRISIS

- Cut back drastically on
  —Labor,
  —Outside services,
  —Manufacturing overhead services.
- Do not approach shareholders for more capital.
- Renegotiate short-term liabilities with the banks.

Identity signals   A third technique involves the use of identity signals—words that assert that something already mentioned is still under discussion.

FREQUENTLY USED IDENTITY SIGNALS	
Identity signal	**Example**
Pronouns	On Monday the division managers will meet to plan the XYZ proposal. **They** will discuss bids, schedules, and contracts.
Repeated words and phrases	The secretary's primary **concern** is with overload on the switchboard. The sales representatives share his **concern** because they have had to deal with client complaints.
Demonstrative adjectives	Each profit center showed signficant improvement in its bottom line. **These** profits did not surprise the controller because she had changed the overhead allocation.

4. Appropriate length

A final characteristic of effective document and paragraph writing is appropriate length. Respect your readers' time; don't make them wade through unnecessary information.

The document   How long should the document be? Theatrical producer David Bellasco proclaims, "If you can't fit your idea on the back of my calling card, you don't have a clear idea." Many managers insist, "My boss refuses to read any memo over one page long." Some writing instructors suggest the KISS formula: "Keep It Short, Stupid." Although these claims may be exaggerated, their underlying idea is sound: limit your document to essential information only.

Each paragraph   How long should a paragraph be? There is no definite answer, but you should avoid the extremes of some journalism (one-sentence paragraphs) and some fiction (chapter-long paragraphs). Vary your length, but usually average no more than: (1) about 150 to 200 words, (2) five sentences, or (3) about 1½ inches of single-spaced typing.

The following examples illustrate the problems associated with inappropriate paragraph length:

SHORT PARAGRAPHS

Poor

If you consistently write in very short paragraphs, you will find they do not develop your ideas.

Short paragraphs also tend to give the impression that you can't group your ideas together logically. Of course the preceding sentence belongs in the first paragraph with a topic sentence about the drawbacks of short paragraphs.

Perhaps after that topic sentence, you could list the drawbacks.

Better

Consistently writing very short paragraphs presents several drawbacks for your reader. First, your paragraphs will lack development. Second, they will lead your reader to think you cannot group your ideas together logically.

The preceding paragraph is now the correct length for the amount of information it contains. The topic sentence introduces the idea of the drawbacks; the subordinate sentences list them. Naturally, that list could have been extended to include several more items.

LONG PARAGRAPHS

Poor

If you consistently write very long paragraphs, your reader may just look at the page and say "Forget it! Why should I wade through all the material to pick out the important points?" And why should your reader do that work? Isn't it your job as a writer to decide what you want to emphasize and to make that stand out? Besides which, the format, or way your ideas appear on the page, is very important psychologically to your reader—or lack of reader. You may want to show the creative gushing process you go through as a writer and just go on and on writing as ideas come into your head. Your psychologist, your friends, or your family might possibly be very interested in how this process works. On the other hand, I doubt very much that the person reading your memo cares too much about your internal processes. The business reader wants to see your main ideas quickly and to have the work of sorting out done for him or her. Didn't you find that just the look of this paragraph rather put you off? Did it make you want to read on? Or did it make you want to give up?

Better

Medium-sized sections (or paragraphs) are easier for your reader to comprehend if you have:

- emphasized your main ideas;
- shown specific results, not a gushing thought process;
- eliminated repetitious ideas; and
- displayed your organizational pattern by highlighting.

II. EFFECTIVE SENTENCES AND WORDS

One of the biggest problems in business and professional writing is lack of clarity. Murky, unclear writing is in turn caused by long, lifeless, pretentious words and sentences. This section offers some suggestions for improving your writing at the sentence and word level by checking for: (1) brevity, (2) vigor, (3) appropriate length, and (4) simplicity.

1. Brevity

Use these four techniques to achieve brevity in your sentences: (1) avoid overused impersonal openings; (2) avoid overused prepositions; (3) avoid compound prepositions; and (4) avoid repetitious phrasing.

Avoid overused impersonal openings   Watch for overuse of impersonal openings in your writing. Although such openings do not always lead to unnecessarily long sentences, probably close to 75 percent of them can be eliminated.

IMPERSONAL OPENINGS		
It is	There is	This is
It was	There was	This was

EXAMPLE: IMPERSONAL OPENING

It was clear to the supervisor on what basis the request for her promotion had been made.

Impersonal opening: It was   *Word count:* 17

The supervisor knew why they wanted to promote her.

No impersonal opening   *Word count:* 9

Avoid overused prepositions   Prepositions are not always bad. Over-using them, however, often produces unnecessarily long sentences. Try circling all the prepositions in a sample page of your writing; if you consistently find more than four in a sentence, you need to revise and shorten. *Of* is usually the worst offender.

MOST PREVALENT PREPOSITIONS

across	for	over
after	from	through
as	in	to
at	in regard to	together
because of	like	under
before	near	until
between	of	up
by	on	with

EXAMPLE: OVERUSED PREPOSITIONS

Central **to** our understanding **of** the problem **of** the organizational structure **in** the XYZ division **of** the ABC Company is the chain **of** command **between** the position **of** the division vice-president, which is not connected **to** all **of** the subordinate departments.

Prepositions: 10   *Word count:* 41
Of: 5

The organizational problem **at** the ABC Company's XYZ division centers **in** the unclear connection **between** the division vice-president and the subordinate departments.

Prepositions: 3   *Word count:* 22
Of: 0

Avoid compound prepositions   In addition to overused prepositions, beware of compound prepositions. These are groups of prepositional words you can easily shorten to one word. Here is a list of compound phrases to avoid.

COMPOUND PREPOSITIONS	
Write	**Avoid**
about	in regard to, in the matter of, with reference to, in relation to, with regard to, in reference to
after	after the conclusion of, in future points in time, subsequent to
although	despite the fact that, notwithstanding the fact that
because, since	accounted for by the fact that, as a result of, due to the fact that, inasmuch as, in the event that, for the reason that, in view of the fact that, on the grounds that, owing to the fact that
before	in advance of, prior to, previous to
by, under	by means of, by virtue of, in accordance with, on the basis of
for	in favor of, for the period of, for the purpose of
if	in the event that
in	in terms of
later	at a later date
like, another	along the lines of, an additional, in addition to, in the nature of, similar to
near	in the proximity of
now, then	as of this date, at the present time, as of this writing, at this/that time, at this/that point in time
on	on the occasion of
soon	at an early date, in the very near future
to	in order to, for the purpose of, so as to, with a view toward
until	until such time as
when, during	at the point in time, at such time, at which time, as soon as, during the course of, during the time that, during the period of time, on the occasion of, until such date as
whether	as to whether, the question as to whether
with	accompanied by, in connection with

Avoid repetitious phrasing Besides watching your prepositions, avoid repetition. Many writers in business and the professions waste words by using repetitious phrasing. Here is a list of repetitious phrases to watch for in managerial writing.

REPETITIOUS PHRASES

absolutely complete	enclosed herewith	numerous and
active considerations	end result	sundry
actual truth	entirely complete	past history
alter or change	exactly identical	personal opinion
assemble together	final outcome	potential
attached hereto	first and foremost	opportunity
basic fundamentals	follows after	reduce down
causal factor	free and clear	refer back
cease and desist	full and complete	repeat again
collect together	future plans	return back
complete stop	great majority	true and correct
consensus of opinion	important essentials	very unique
contributing factor	integral part	visible to the eye
dollar amount	midway between	vitally essential
each and every	new changes	

Although an expression such as *very unique* is always repetitious, some expressions are sometimes repetitious. Beware of the following twelve potentially repetitious wordings: *area* (as in *the area of communication;* write *communication*), *basis* (as in *fee-for-service basis;* write *fee-for-service*), *character* (as in *skills of a professional character;* write *professional skills*), *context* (as in *in a business context;* write *in business*), *degree* (as in *the degree of the staff's commitment;* write *staff's commitment*), *field* (as in *the legal field;* write *law*), *level* (as in *at the management level;* write *management*), *nature* (as in *behavior of an uncooperative nature;* write *uncooperative behavior*), *sphere* (as in *within the sphere of their division;* write *within their division*), *situation* (as in *problem situation;* write *problem*), *who* (as in *Min, who is an attorney;* write *Min, an attorney*), and *which* (as in *St. Louis, which is where;* write *St. Louis, where*).

2. Vigor

Much business and professional writing is lifeless, boring, and wordy, not merely because it is too long, but because it lacks vigor. Vigorous writing demands effective verbs. This section offers four suggestions for adding punch to your writing: (1) avoid overusing nouns; (2) avoid elongated verbs; (3) avoid overused weak linking verbs; and (4) avoid overused passive verbs.

Throughout this section on vigorous verbs, I will cite as examples variations on this sentence:

Rockefeller kicked the cat.

That concise sentence contains a vigorous verb, *kicked*, and only four words. Contrast it with the examples that follow.

Avoid overusing nouns   One way to add vigor to your writing is to avoid overusing nouns at the expense of verbs. Nouns, of course, are useful and necessary; verbs, however, give language its life and movement. In our example sentence, we move from two nouns (*Rockefeller* and *cat*) and four words total to five nouns and 12 words total:

Rockefeller engaged in kicking activity in the vicinity of the cat's position.

Number of nouns: 5   *Word count:* 12

Although this example may seem somewhat fanciful, noun phrases such as "motorized attendance modules" (buses) and interior "intrusion detection systems" (burglar alarms) have appeared in published writing, causing writing expert Richard Wydick to advise "noun chain confusion avoidance techniques."

Avoid elongated verbs   Prefer concise verbs to elongated verbs—phrases made up of a verb plus a noun plus a preposition. In the next example sentence, *kicked,* a concise verb, becomes an elongated verb form, *made kicking motions toward.* This change increases the number of words in the sentence from four to seven:

> Rockefeller made kicking motions toward the cat.
>
> *Elongated verb form:* made kicking motions toward
> *Word count:* 7

Although this example may also seem fanciful, take a look at the very common business and professional examples listed in the following table. Since elongated verbs always include a noun, watch out for words ending with *-ment, -ion, -tion, -ance, -ency, -ancy, -ant,* and *-ent.*

EXAMPLES OF ELONGATED VERBS

Prefer concise verbs	Avoid elongated verbs (verb plus noun plus preposition)
analyze	perform an analysis of
act	take action on
assume	make assumptions about
can	be in a position to
change	effect a change in
conclude	reach a conclusion about
consider	give consideration to
correct	is corrective of
decide	make a decision regarding
depends	is dependent on
end	bring to an end
examine	make an examination of
know	to be cognizant of
order	place an order for
realize	make a realization that
recommend	make a recommendation that
reduce	effect a reduction in
tend	exhibit a tendency to

Avoid overused weak linking verbs Elongated verbs often result in concurrent overuse of weak linking verbs. When writers take the active force in a sentence (such as the verb *kick*) and make it into a noun (such as *kicking situation*), they take away the verb's energy, producing a sentence such as:

A kicking situation is taking place between Rockefeller and the cat.

Weak linking verb: is   *Word count:* 11
Noun form: kicking situation

Linking verbs are the dozen or so verbs that take a complement. The main ones are:

LINKING VERBS

be   look   appear
become   seem   sound
                                              feel

Here are two other examples of how weak linking verbs produce wordy, lifeless sentences:

Plan A **is** successful in terms of production.

Weak linking verb: is   *Word count:* 8
Noun: production

Plant A produces well.

Forceful verb: produces   *Word count:* 4

There **appears** to be a tendency on the part of investment bankers. . . .

Weak linking verb: appears   *Word count:* 12
Noun: tendency

Investment bankers tend. . . .

Forceful verb: tend   *Word count:* 3

Avoid overused passive verbs   Overused passive verbs are a certain kind of weak verb especially prevalent in business and professional writing. Passive constructions also always include or imply action done *by* somebody or something. When writers take the active agent in a sentence (such as *Rockefeller*) and make it the object of the sentence (such as *by Rockefeller*), they have a passive sentence:

> The cat was kicked by Rockefeller.
>
> > *Passive verb:* was kicked by   *Word count:* 6
> > *Passive subject:* cat (receives action, does not perform it)

Sometimes, of course, passive voice is appropriate, but its habitual, unthinking overuse can lead to problems. Passive constructions are (1) usually more wordy, (2) usually more weighty and formal, and (3) often unclear about placing responsibility.

Here are some examples demonstrating these problems:

> They **were** not **told by** anyone.
>
> > *Passive:* usually more wordy
>
> Nobody told them.
>
> > *Active:* less wordy

> A fair decision **was rendered** difficult **by** the Chair's evident bias.
>
> > *Passive:* unnecessarily weighty and formal
>
> The Chair's evident bias made it hard for her to decide fairly.
>
> > *Active:* less weighty and formal

> It **is urged** that special study be given to the recommendations in this report.
>
> > *Passive:* unclear who is urging
>
> We urge you to give special study to the recommendations in this report.
>
> > *Active:* urged by the Task Force

3. Appropriate length

Long, complicated sentences are harder for your reader to comprehend than shorter, simpler sentences. How long is too long? One well-known readability formula recommends that sentences average 17 words. Other experts recommend 20 to 25 words. And most experts agree you should reconsider sentences over 40 to 50 words. But writing is not like accounting: you cannot judge sentence length by any hard-and-fast rule. Rather, your sentence is too long any time its length makes it confusing.

The problems   Beware especially of two kinds of sentences that tend to be ponderously long. *Overly compound sentences* join too many main ideas together, usually with the word *and*.

EXAMPLE: OVERLY COMPOUND SENTENCE

Poor
> Sufficient computer technology exists for our needs, and we should direct our efforts toward applying such technology efficiently, and the emphasis should be on the accounting system and the inventory of the warehouses.

Better
> Since sufficient computer technology exists for our needs, we should direct our efforts toward applying such technology efficiently. We should emphasize two applications: the accounting system and the warehouse inventory.

Another problem is *overly complex sentences*—sentences that pile up phrases, parenthetical ideas, and qualifiers to the point where the reader has trouble excavating the main idea.

EXAMPLE: OVERLY COMPLEX SENTENCE

Poor
> The effect of foreign competition also shows up in the downward trend for widget exports, which, during the first four months of this year, averaged about 433 per capita, compared with an average of 628 per capita during the same period last year.

Better
> The effect of foreign competition also shows up in the downward trend for widget exports. During the first four months of this year, we sold 433 widgets per capita. During the same period last year, we sold 628 widgets per capita.

The solutions   If you find consistent strings of overly long sentences in your writing, break them up with transitions, internal enumeration, or bullet points.

EXAMPLES: SOLUTIONS TO OVERLY LONG SENTENCES

Poor

Regardless of their seniority, all employees who hope to be promoted will continue their education either by enrolling in the special courses to be offered by the ABC Company, scheduled to be given on the next eight Saturdays beginning on January 24, or by taking approved correspondence courses selected from a list available in the Staff Development Office.

Better

Using transitions

Regardless of their seniority, all employees who hope to be promoted will continue their education in one of two ways. First, they may enroll in the special courses offered by the ABC Company, scheduled to be given on the next eight Saturdays beginning January 24. Second, they may take approved correspondence courses selected from a list available in the Staff Development Office.

Using internal enumeration

Regardless of their seniority, all employees who hope to be promoted will continue their education by either (1) enrolling in the special courses offered oy the ABC Company, scheduled to be given on the next eight Saturdays beginning on January 24, or (2) taking approved correspondence courses selected from a list available in the Staff Development Office.

Using bullet points

Regardless of their seniority, all employees who hope to be promoted will continue their education in one of two ways:

- by enrolling in the special courses offered by the ABC Company, scheduled to be given on the next eight Saturdays beginning on January 24, or
- by taking approved correspondence courses selected from a list available in the Staff Development Office.

Variety and rhythm   Good sentence length, however, is more subtle than merely limiting your sentences to a constant 20 to 25 words. A lack of variety in sentence length or structure can be just as deadening as strings of long sentences. Therefore, watch out for short, monotonous, identically structured sentences.

EXAMPLE: MONOTONOUS SENTENCE STRUCTURE

Poor

> We should invest in plastics research immediately. We should build and staff three research laboratories. We should expand our involvement in scientific associations. We must not let research overshadow our practical image. That image should be preserved through advertising campaigns.

Better

> We should invest in plastics research immediately by (1) building and staffing three research laboratories and (2) expanding our involvement in scientific associations. Research, however, must not overshadow our practical image, which we will continue to reinforce in our advertising campaign.

Sentence lengths: 21 words, 17 words

Perhaps the most subtle concept of all in sentence length is the concept of rhythm. No rule can standardize this concept. Instead, you must rely on an intuitive guide—how the sentence sounds. In the following example, the improved version allows your voice to rise and fall naturally. It has rhythm, like spoken English.

EXAMPLE: LACK OF RHYTHM

Poor

> Each person to whom this memo is written is entitled to submit, or request his or her supervisor to submit, to the Personnel Department at the address above, a request for reconsideration of the question as to whether he or she should have been considered for internal promotion.

Better

> You or your supervisor may write to the Personnel Department if you think you should have been considered for an internal promotion.

4. Simplicity

A final way to improve clarity in your writing is to use short, familiar words instead of long, pretentious ones. Of course, nothing is wrong with any big word, provided it is: (1) necessary for efficient communication and (2) appropriate for your audience. In the words of writing expert Robert Gunning, "Write to express, not to impress."

EXAMPLES: POMPOUS WORDS

Write	Avoid
about	pursuant to
affect, influence	impact on
appear	materialize
around	periphery
aware	be cognizant of
begin	commence, initiate
best	optimal
common	commonality
cost	fiscal expenditures
discuss	interface with
end	terminate
get the facts	ascertain the data
here, there	herein, therein
improve	ameliorate
legal limit	obligational limitation
limits	parameters
me	the undersigned
order, require	mandate
pay	remunerate
people	individuals
prevent	obviate
previous	aforementioned
send	forward, transmit
shortage	insufficiency
stop	render inoperative
this	the aforementioned
until	pending determination of
use	utilize, utilization of

EXAMPLES: POMPOUS PHRASES

Write	Avoid
about	pursuant to, in reference to
around	in the periphery of
as you asked,	per your request/per our discussion,
as you requested,	pursuant to your request/our discussion,
as we discussed	as per your request/our discussion,
	in accordance with your request,
	in compliance with your request
here are/here is	enclosed please find,
	attached hereto please find
if you need more help	should additional assistance be required
separately	under separate cover
until	pending determination of

A classic example of pretentious language comes from George Orwell's "Politics and the English Language." First he quotes a passage from Ecclesiastes:

> I returned and saw under the sun, that the race is not to the swift, nor the battle to the strong, neither yet bread to the wise, nor yet riches to men of understanding, nor yet favour to men of skill; but time and chance happeneth to them all.

Then he writes it in inflated, multisyllabic jargon:

> Objective consideration of contemporary phenomena compels the conclusion that success or failure in competitive activities exhibits no tendency to be commensurate with innate capacity, but that a considerable element of the unpredictable must invariably be taken into account.

As Orwell concludes:

> Never use a foreign phrase, a scientific word or a jargon word if you can think of an everyday English equivalent.

CHECKLIST
WRITING: THE PRODUCT

I. Effective documents and paragraphs
1. Organization: Have you provided a hierarchy of ideas and ordered your ideas clearly? Have you organized each paragraph around one generalization stated as a topic sentence (for each paragraph) or as subheading (for a section)? Have you ordered your paragraphs clearly?
2. Unity and emphasis: Have you omitted extraneous material? Have you emphasized your points with a good introduction and conclusion? Have you omitted any sentence in each paragraph that does not amplify the generalizing topic sentence or subheading? Have you emphasized your topic sentence or subheading by placing it at the beginning of the paragraph or section?
3. Coherence: Have you clearly bridged between your paragraphs and between the sentences within each paragraph by using transitions, highlighting, or identity signals?
4. Appropriate length: Have you limited yourself to essential information? Have you varied your length, but generally averaged no more than 200 to 300 words, five sentences, or 1½ inches of single-spaced typing?

II. Effective sentences and words
1. Brevity: Have you avoided overused impersonal openings (such as *It is/was, There is/was, This is/was*), overused prepositions, and compound prepositions? Have you eliminated repetitious phrasing?
2. Vigor: Have you avoided overusing nouns? Have you avoided elongated verbs (that is, verb + noun + preposition), overused weak linking verbs (such as *be, become, look, seem, appear, sound, feel*), and overused passive verbs (that is, verbs that express action done *by* somebody or something)?
3. Appropriate length: Have you broken up long sentences with transitions, internal enumeration, or bullet points?
4. Simplicity: Have you avoided unnecessarily pompous words and phrases?

IV

OUTLINE
SPEAKING: THE PROCESS

I. Prepare your presentation.
  1. Use an effective opening.
  2. Include a preview.
  3. Make your major points clear.
  4. Use an effective closing.

II. Prepare to handle other speaking situations.
  1. Meetings
  2. Question-and-answer periods
  3. Listening and discussion sessions
  4. Introductions and team presentations
  5. Manuscript and impromptu speaking
  6. Media and telecommunications

III. Select your visual aids.
  1. Compose your visual aid content.
  2. Choose your visual aid equipment.

IV

SPEAKING:
THE PROCESS

Like good writing, good oral presentations must be clearly and logically organized. If you are unfamiliar with how to organize your material clearly, see Chapter II before continuing here.

Once you have your material organized, however, presenting it orally is quite a different matter from presenting it in writing. Make the most of the advantages inherent in speaking, outlined in the checklist at the end of Chapter I: the opportunities to build a group identity, to establish group relationships, and to receive a group response.

This chapter covers the process of preparing an oral presentation. The first section concerns preparing a standard presentation. The second section covers preparing how to handle other speaking situations, such as question-and-answer sessions and meetings. The third deals with preparing your visual aids.

I. PREPARE YOUR PRESENTATION

Presenting information orally differs from presenting it in writing. An effective presentation structure includes: (1) an opening, (2) a preview, (3) limited major points, and (4) a closing. Decisions regarding each of these characteristics will depend on your managerial style, as explained in Chapter I: tell/sell for higher speaker control and lower audience involvement; consult/join for lower speaker control and higher audience involvement.

1. Use an effective opening

The audience memory curve illustrated in Chapter I emphasized the importance of your opening. In speaking, however, your opening is even more crucial than in writing: you must arouse your listeners' interest; you must establish your credibility and rapport. An effective opening stimulates your listeners' vital interests; it answers their question, "Why should I be listening to this, anyway?"

Regardless of the kind of opening you select, always start with a "grabber."

EFFECTIVE OPENINGS		
Managerial style		**Opening**
Any style	Refer to the unusual	Rhetorical question Anticipatory promise of what you will discuss Vivid image Startling example or story Important statistic
	Refer to the familiar	Audience (who they are) Occasion (why you are there) Relationship between the audience and the subject Something or someone familiar to the audience

2. Include a preview

A preview is an agenda, an outline, an idea of where you are going with your presentation. Think about the contrast between listeners and readers. Your readers can skim a document, see how long it is, and read your headings and subheadings before they start reading. Your listeners, on the other hand, have no idea what you will be covering unless you tell them. One of the most common problems in business presentations is the lack of a preview. Always state a preview explicitly before you begin discussing your main points.

In the most formal situations, a preview might sound like this: "In the next twenty minutes, I will discuss sales in each of three regions: the Southeast, the Far West, and the Midwest." On less formal occasions, your preview might be: "I'd like to go over the sales figures in three regions." In any situation, the point of the preview is to give your audience a skeleton, a very general outline, of what you will be discussing.

EFFECTIVE PREVIEWS	
Managerial style	**Preview**
Tell	List your three to five main points: listeners definitely remember better if they hear an overview first.
Sell	State the problem or need you will remedy; state your organizational structure.
Consult/join	State major objectives, areas of discussion, and approximate amount of time you will spend on each area.

3. Make your major points clear

Listeners cannot process as much information as readers, do not stay oriented as easily as readers, and do not remember information they hear only once. Therefore, make the points in your presentation very clear by: (1) limiting your main points, (2) using explicit transitions, and (3) using internal summaries.

CLEAR MAJOR POINTS

Managerial style	Major points
Tell/sell	Limit yourself to three to five major points: group your complex ideas into three to five major areas.
Consult/join	Separate clearly between two kinds of activity: 1. Discussion: draw out listeners; postpone evaluation and criticism; encourage free and creative thinking. 2. Debate and consensus: encourage critical thinking, argument, debate; reach consensus; determine next action.

Managerial style	Explicit transitions
Tell/sell	Use between your major points, to reinforce learning: Say "The second recommendation is," not "Second"; Say "Another benefit of the systems is," not "In addition."
Consult/join	Use between your major sections: Say "The third area we need to discuss this morning is," not "Next."

Managerial Style	Internal summaries
Tell/sell	Summarize between your major points or subpoints.
Consult/join	Summarize consensus between your two major organizational sections.

4. Use an effective closing

Your audience is likely to remember your last words. So avoid the "Well, that's all I have to say," "I guess that's about it" syndrome. Use a strong, obvious transitional phrase—such as "to summarize" or "in conclusion"—to introduce your closing remarks, and you will see nonverbal signs that your audience is perking up. If you have a question-and-answer period (see pp. 87–89), be sure to save a few minutes at the end for your conclusions. In any event, use an effective closing.

EFFECTIVE CLOSINGS

Managerial style	Closing
Tell	List your three to five major points. (You may feel as though you're being repetitive, but this kind of reinforcement is extremely effective for explaining or instructing.) Refer to the rhetorical question, promise, image, or story you used in your opening.
Sell	Call for action based on what you have presented; make the "What next?" step explicit. Refer to the benefits your audience will receive from following the advice in your presentation.
Consult/join	List the main points you have come up with as a group; make sure you reach a consensus; make sure your audience can see the results of the time they have spent.

II. PREPARE TO HANDLE
OTHER SPEAKING SITUATIONS

So far, we have looked at the process of preparing a presentation. In business and the professions, however, you may also find yourself in other speaking situations. This section offers some additional techniques for dealing with other kinds of speaking: (1) meetings, (2) question-and-answer periods, (3) listening and discussion sessions, (4) introductions and team presentations, (5) impromptu and manuscript speaking, and (6) media interviews and telecommunications.

1. Meetings

Meetings are very different from standard business presentations. Usually, in a presentation *you* are primarily presenting information, either to inform or to persuade. In a meeting, on the other hand, *a group* of people is solving a problem or accomplishing a task.

Chairing a meeting involves two very different kinds of skills. One set of skills has to do with accomplishing the *task*, the goal at hand. The other set of skills is usually referred to as running the *process*—that is, getting people to participate. Experts in meeting management disagree on whether it is possible for one person to fulfill both the task and the process functions. The traditional view is yes, it is possible. Many contemporary experts, however, suggest separating the roles. They feel that one person—usually called a "facilitator" instead of a chairperson or leader—should run the process, and that he or she should be concerned only with keeping things running smoothly.

Task functions   The task functions for the leader include: deciding on an agenda (the tasks you are going to try to accomplish), deciding how you are going to discuss issues, and deciding how you are going to reach a decision.

1. Agenda   The first task function is preparing an agenda. Include both a starting and finishing time, usually no longer than two hours apart. Place important ideas first or last; do not bury them in the middle. If wasting time on trivial items is a potential problem, schedule tentative times for each item on the agenda. Differentiate the goals for each agenda item: for your information, for discussion, for a decision. As a general rule, distribute the agenda two or three days in advance. Thus, participants will have enough time to prepare, but not enough time to lose or forget about the agenda.

2. Discussion   The second task function is deciding how the group will discuss issues. One discussion procedure is called the *reflective-thinking model* or the *problem-solving model*. In this process, the group (1) defines the problem specifically, (2) analyzes the problems—looks at information, policies, the organizational scheme, the data, (3) determines standards or criteria by which it will measure any solution, (4) lists possible solutions, (5) selects the best solution, and (6) decides how to implement that solution.

Another procedure is called the *nominal-group model*. This is an unusual, but increasingly popular, way of making sure all people participate. In this procedure, the participants (1) list their ideas independently, not talking with other group members, (2) compile a group list, recording one item from each person's list until all are included, (3) revise the group list to reword, combine, or avoid duplicates, (4) rank the master list independently (perhaps only the top three to five items), and (5) collate the results.

A third decision-making process is called *brainstorming*. The most important key to success in a brainstorming session is to divide the session into two distinct stages. During stage one, the group simply records ideas; it does not evaluate, react to, or decide on any ideas. Everyone blurts out any and every association that comes to mind. No one is allowed to criticize or evaluate the ideas. It is very important to record *all* the ideas as they are stated. Usually, this recording is done on flip charts or the blackboard. During stage two, the group reviews the list of ideas, grouping related ideas and striking irrelevant ones. From this more organized list, the group can work on reaching a decision.

3. *Decision*   This brings us to the final task function: how you will resolve the issues you have discussed. Having finished the discussion, how will you decide what to do? One option is a *one-person decision*—either the chairperson or the person "in charge." Here, the purpose of the group is to serve as an advisory board. Naturally, the participants should be told in advance who will be making the final decision.

A second—and probably the most familiar—option is decision by *majority rule*. According to parliamentary procedure, a decision or resolution is offered in the form of a motion. Another person must second the motion. Participants cannot ignore a motion: they may debate it, amend it, or vote on it. In addition to these kinds of content motions, parliamentary procedure includes various procedural motions. For example, you can make a motion to curtail debate, to set a motion aside, to clarify a procedure, or to repeal a passed motion. Each procedure is slightly different: some require "seconds," some do not; some are debatable; some are amendable; some need a simple majority to pass, others a two-thirds majority.

Both one-person decision and majority rule are especially useful when the decision is not that important or when there are severe time pressures. The problem with these ways of making group decisions is that some people may feel left out, ignored, or defeated. The third and fourth options for decision making—consensus and unanimity— may be more appropriate when decisions are very important or when you need everyone's support to implement the motion.

The third option—one that is becoming increasingly popular in business meetings—is decision by *consensus*. Consensus develops when the group reaches a decision that may not be everybody's first choice, but that each person is willing to agree to and implement. Consensus usually involves hearing all points of view and incorporating these viewpoints into the solution. Also, consensus is usually not reached by vote, but rather by agreement. For example, the chairperson might ask all participants, "Do you feel comfortable with this solution?" Or, if one person seems to be the lone holdout for a position, "Well, Leonard, we understand your argument clearly, but the rest of us don't want that solution. Can you live with this one instead?"

The final option—*unanimity*—is very rarely used in business meetings. Unanimity means that the decision is the first choice of everyone present—unlike the compromise implied by consensus. Unanimity, therefore, gives each participant veto power and may drag on the decision making. It is appropriate only in extremely important decisions or when everyone is committed to the possibility of this process working.

Process functions   Whereas task functions are concerned with reaching decisions about accomplishing your goal, process functions are concerned with making sure everyone participates. Here are five process functions to keep in mind.

1. Show support   To do a good job of facilitating the group process, remember that supporting others' right to speak does not necessarily mean you agree with them. Instead, it means you respect them, accept them, and allow them to express their opinions. Responses that might show your support include "That idea shows a lot of thought. What do the rest of you think?" or "Let's consider what Jeanne has just recommended." Responses that do not show your support for someone's right to speak, on the other hand, include "I disagree" or "That's wrong, because. . . ."

2. Encourage diversity   A good facilitator encourages diversity of opinions. A group can make better decisions if they have a wider range of options. You'll never discover that range if everyone agrees with one another all the time. Some experts even claim that groups make better decisions when there is more diversity.

3. Encourage participation   Having shown support and encouraged diversity, you can encourage participation by using the listening skills we shall discuss on pp. 90–91. For example, you can ask open-ended questions, questions that cannot be answered "Yes" or "No." You will be more likely to increase participation if you ask "What do you think of this idea" rather than "Do you like this idea?"

4. Avoid dominance Another process function is to avoid dominance by any one person—you or someone else. To control yourself, avoid interrupting; don't talk for more than a couple of minutes; keep asking the other people to contribute; ask someone else to present background information; and hold your opinions until the end. To control others—especially those with high status or authority who tend to talk too much and interrupt more often—avoid a direct confrontation in front of the group. Instead, try talking to such people outside the meeting. If that doesn't work, try nonverbal signs—such as attention and visible signs of approval to other people trying to get a word in. As a next step, try a tactful but firm interruption, such as "Excuse me, Elenora, but we need to keep our remarks brief so everyone has the chance to talk" or "That's a good point, Nick. I'd like to hear what the others think of it." Another technique is to place the disrupter at your side and call on him or her minimally. Finally, you might try giving the disrupter a job to do—keeping the minutes, chairing a subcommittee. This may provide the status or recognition that many disrupters are looking for.

5. Control conflict Finally, avoid hostile conflict among group members. Conflict of ideas is healthy in groups; conflict of personalities is not. If hostile conflict arises, summarize or paraphrase the different viewpoints, emphasizing the places where people agree. Also, be sure to keep the discussion focused on ideas, not on attacking people. Instead of asking other participants to choose sides, try to work toward a solution that allows all sides to win and maintain their pride.

2. Question-and-answer periods

Some speeches or presentations include give and take between speakers and their audiences in the form of a question-and-answer period. Handling audience questions involves deciding when to take questions, how to take questions, and how to deal with difficult questioners.

When to take questions You should definitely control this issue. Do not let your audience either overrun your presentation with questions or hold back unnecessarily if they do not understand a key point. Make your stance clear from the start. Say, for example, "Please feel free to ask questions as they come up," or "Please hold all your questions until the end of the presentation," or "Feel free to interrupt with questions of understanding or clarification, but since we only have an hour together, please hold questions of debate or discussion until the end."

Unless, of course, the format for a question-and-answer period is already set for you, consider the following advantages and disadvantages when you decide whether to take questions during or after your presentation.

If you take questions *during* the presentation, the questions will be more meaningful to the questioner, the feedback more immediate to you, and your audience may listen more actively. On the other hand, questions during the presentation can upset your schedule, waste time, and introduce information prematurely. To alleviate these problems, (1) when you plan, allow enough time for questions, (2) control digressions, and (3) make it clear you will discuss an issue later rather than introduce it prematurely.

If you take questions *after* the presentation, you will control the schedule and the flow of information. On the other hand, you risk losing your audience's attention and even comprehension if they cannot interrupt with their questions. Since audiences tend to remember more material from the beginning and the end of a presentation, however, having "Q and A" last places undue emphasis on the question period. To alleviate this problem, save time for a two-to-three-minute summary after the question period.

How to take questions   Once you've established when to take questions, prepare yourself for how you will take them. Before questions even come up, you can prepare yourself by controlling your attitude. Avoid a defensive attitude. Instead, think of it as a compliment that your listeners are interested enough to ask for clarification, amplification, or justification. You can also prepare by anticipating possible questions. Try to guess what the questions will be. Bring along extra information—perhaps even extra visual aids—to answer them. Another way to anticipate questions is to ask a colleague to play devil's advocate during your rehearsal.

During the session itself, keep everyone involved by calling on people from various locations throughout the audience. Once someone asks a question, be sure you understand it before you answer. Paraphrase complicated questions to make sure you're on the right track. If the group is large, paraphrase or repeat all questions to be sure everyone in the audience hears them. Then, decide how to answer, always keeping your communication objective in mind. Try to divert the question back to your main ideas. Even if you know a lot of information for your answer, limit yourself to that which advances your objective.

Based on your communication objective, then, answer the question. What if someone asks a question you don't understand? Say "I'm sorry. I don't understand the question," not "Your question isn't clear." What if someone asks a question you had planned to cover later in your talk? Make it clear you will get to that point later instead of divulging premature information.

When you answer questions, avoid getting into a one-to-one conversation with a single member of the audience. Therefore, unless someone looks extremely confused, avoid asking for approval of your answer, such as by inquiring "Does that answer your question?" Remember to maintain eye contact with the entire audience, not just with the person who asked the question. Also, avoid ending your answer by looking right at the questioner: he or she may feel invited to ask another question.

How to answer difficult questioners Although most people will be genuinely interested in understanding or reacting to your presentation, you may occasionally encounter difficult questioners—people trying to show off, gain control, and so forth. Try these possible strategies for answering them.

The first step in answering difficult questioners is to compliment them. For example, say "Good question. Let's explore that in more detail after the presentation is over," or "That's an interesting point. I wish we had more time to discuss it."

The second step is to divert the question. Here are five types of distressing questioners, and how to divert their questions back onto your track. (1) Show-offs who want to talk themselves: control their answer time or invite them to talk after the presentation. (2) Hotshots who ask loaded questions: ask how they would answer the question. (3) Gossips who ask personal questions: make the irrelevance clear; don't answer, or depersonalize the question and answer in more general terms. (4) Windbags who ask long, rambling questions: paraphase to shorten the question, then answer, or invite them to talk after the presentation. (5) Controllers who ask questions that focus on their own interests only: direct your answer back to your communication objective.

How to buy time If you are momentarily stymied by a question, here are some techniques to buy you some thinking time: (1) Repeat: "You're wondering how to deal with this situation." (2) Turn around: "How would *you* deal with this situation?" (3) Turn outward: "How would the rest of you deal with this situation?" (4) Reflect: "Good question. Let's think about that for a moment." (5) Write: If you are using a suitable visual aid, write down the main point of the question as you think.

3. Listening and discussion sessions

In many business and professional speaking situations, you are not merely presenting information, perhaps with limited audience interchange, but you are interacting to elicit information from others. Such interactions may include brainstorming, interviewing, reviewing job performance, collecting data, resolving conflict, and participating in certain meetings. In all such situations, you must listen to others. In fact, various studies indicate that business and professional people spend from 45 to 75 percent of their time listening.

Therefore, your ability to listen well and to elicit information from others is crucial to your professional success. The benefits you gain from good listening are tremendous: you receive more detailed information, which will enable you to make better decisions; you increase your understanding so you can solve problems better; and you increase cooperation so you can improve working relationships and improve your chances for effective implementation. The following techniques that deal with how to look, feel, think, and speak are designed to make you a better listener.

The way you look   Effective listeners show their interest by looking and acting interested. To look alert, maintain good eye contact, posture, facial expression, and voice energy. Show your interest by nodding your head and using brief encouragers, such as "I see," "Yes," or "Uh-huh." On the other hand, avoid such obvious signs of rudeness as reading, looking at your watch, or gazing out the window.

At the same time, remove any physical distractions. Get rid of anything that might distract you or the talker. Avoid doodling, tapping your pencil, shuffling paper, or fidgeting with your glasses, rings, and so forth.

The way you feel   Empathize with the person to whom you're listening. Try to put yourself in his or her position to create a climate of understanding. Such a climate will lead to a true exchange of information. At the same time, be patient. Give the talker time. Good ideas are not necessarily spoken quickly and concisely—or even clearly. Avoid interrupting. Finally, hold your fire. Do not block communication by arguing, criticizing, or becoming angry too quickly. Listen first.

The way you think   Try to listen objectively, hearing the person out before you judge. Analyze the speaker's content by listening for main ideas and then organizing those main thoughts as you listen. Also analyze the speaker's feelings. In addition to what the person says, be sensitive to how she or he says it. Listen "between the lines." Be aware of the speaker's tone of voice, volume, facial expression, and body movement.

What you say   First of all, be prepared. Do your homework before the interchange. Prepare for any new terminology or background information. Set your communication strategy, as we discussed in Chapter I. Once the session begins, establish a climate for communication. Start the interaction by putting the talker at ease, perhaps by making small talk briefly. Then state your purpose or objectives.

Clearly, one of the main ways to get people to talk and to show interest is to ask them questions. The questions designed to elicit the most information from others are known as *open-ended* questions— that is, questions that cannot be easily answered with a "Yes" or "No." For example, you are bound to get more extensive responses if you:

Ask	Instead of
Tell me about the computer project.	Is the computer project going well?
How do you feel about your recent job performance?	Are you satisfied with your recent job performance?
What concerns you about the deadlines on this schedule?	Can your staff meet the deadlines on this schedule?

Once you have asked open-ended questions, paraphrase the other person's response. This will enable you to check the accuracy of what you think you have heard, encourage the other person to elaborate on what he or she has said, and show that you are listening. You might paraphrase the important words or summarize the important ideas.

Finally, the most important step toward becoming an effective listener is to stop talking yourself. Unfortunately, most of us prefer talking to listening. But you must stop talking before you can listen.

4. Introductions and team presentations

In some business speaking situations you are not the only one "on stage." This section provides some suggestions for how to introduce a speaker and how to deliver a team presentation.

Introductions   When you are asked to introduce someone who is about to speak, your job is to make the audience want to listen. You want to interest audience members in the topic and increase their respect for the speaker.

1. *Greet the audience and introduce the subject*   An introduction usually starts with your welcoming the audience. Often this initial greeting includes the name of the sponsoring organization, the nature of the gathering, or your name and function. Having greeted the people in your audience, arouse their curiosity by identifying the subject and indicating its importance.

2. *Present the speaker*   The longest part of the introduction should be devoted to creating a favorable impression of the speaker. You can obtain information about the speaker from his or her résumé—or, better yet, from interviewing the speaker. Don't bore your audience by reading every detail on the résumé, however. Instead, be selective: omit information the audience already knows; choose her or his most distinctive qualifications or experiences—those most relevant to this audience and to this occasion. Finally, at the end of your introduction, present the speaker by name.

3. *Keep the introduction short*   Usually, introductions are no longer than five minutes. Generally, the less the speaker is known to your audience, the longer the introduction needs to be. If, for example, you were introducing the president of your company to a group of employees, you might just say, "It's my pleasure to introduce our president, Scott Neslin." If, on the other hand, you were introducing someone the audience did not know, you'd want to include more details.

Team presentations   Team presentations are just like any other presentation in terms of structure, visuals, and so forth. The only difference is that instead of one person delivering the entire presentation, a series of people deliver it. Team presentations are fairly common in business—both because you may want your audience to get to know the entire group of you, and because you may want your team to all receive recognition.

1. Organize as a whole   The major problem with team presentations occurs when each presenter prepares his or her own parts—and the parts never coalesce into a whole. A team presentation is *not* a panel discussion; it is a coherent, organized, whole presentation that just happens to be spoken by various people instead of one person. Therefore, team presentations should be organized as a whole.

2. Provide clear transitions between speakers   For example, one team member might give the introduction and preview, outlining what each subsequent team member will discuss. As each new team member starts, she or he should provide a transition, such as "Now that Mr. Bower has discussed our proposal, I'd like to show you the financial results we can expect if we decide to go ahead with this proposal." Often, the same team member who opened the session returns to deliver the closing.

3. Use visual aids consistently   For one thing, make sure all the visual aids look alike: use the same color coding (for example, blue for all the main headings throughout); use the same typeface and type size throughout. In addition, present the visuals consistently. Stick with one of three options: (1) have each person handle his or her own visuals; (2) have each person take a turn handling them for another speaker; or (3) have one person handle them all throughout.

4. Rehearse as a group   To put together a team presentation that is coherent in its organization, transitions between speakers, and visual aids, the team must meet as a group to structure the presentation, to discuss visual aids, and to divide up speaking responsibilities. The group should also rehearse together. Normally, group presentations involve at least two rehearsals. In a "dry run" rehearsal, run through what you will say and how you will provide transitions, and present rough drafts of your visual aids. Later, stage a full dress rehearsal to perfect your delivery and flow.

5. Avoid typical problems   Two final words of warning about team presentations. One, remember that every member of the team is always "on stage" to the audience. From the moment you walk into the room, the audience is watching each of you. Keep this in mind especially as you are listening to one another speak. Don't yawn, slouch, or whisper to one another unnecessarily. Two, if there is to be a question-and-answer period after the presentation, either assign one person as a moderator to divvy up the questions, or have each person answer automatically all questions in his or her clearly defined area of expertise.

5. Manuscript and impromptu speaking

The kind of presentation we looked at in the first section of this chapter was one that was prepared, but not read word for word. You may find, however, that you are occasionally called upon to speak word for word from a manuscript or to speak off the cuff.

Manuscript speaking The main problem people have in writing manuscript speeches is that they use "written style" instead of "spoken style." A speech in written style may look fine on paper, but it sounds stilted, formal, and pompous. When you write a manuscript speech, then, keep in mind four aspects of spoken style.

First, use appropriate wording. Avoid phrases no one would actually say, phrases that sound stilted or hard to pronounce. For example, you might write "If you were asked to do so," but you would say "If someone asked you to do that."

Second, avoid phrases separating the subject and verb. Your reader can easily follow this sentence: "Linda Argenti, who is currently the president of ABC Company, will be the first speaker on the panel." You make it much easier for a listener, however, if you do not separate the subject from the verb: "President Linda Argenti will be the first speaker on the panel."

Third, use different sentence lengths. Although sentence length—as in regular writing—should vary, in speech writing sentences must break down into shorter units, and you may use sentence fragments.

Finally, rhythm is much more important in spoken style than in written style. Consider, for example, the rhythmic impact of Patrick Henry's famous quotation "Give me liberty or give me death." Contrast this version with the unrhythmic "Give me liberty or death." Similarly, John Kennedy's rhythmic "Ask not what your country can do for you; ask what you can do for your country" is more effective than the unrhythmic "Don't ask what your country can do for you, but what can you do for it."

Keeping these four considerations in mind, write the first draft of your speech. Or, write notes, then record yourself speaking from those notes. The transcript of what you just recorded becomes the draft of the speech. Once you have a draft, edit it and then read it aloud (or have the person for whom you're writing the speech read it aloud). After making any changes necessary, you are ready to type the manuscript in its final form.

A speech manuscript looks different from a regular page of writing. For one thing, it should be typed in large print: some typewriters have *orator* or *presenter* typefaces; some computers will print out extra-bold or extra-large letters. The margins also look strange: leave about one third of the right side of the page blank for notes; leave about one third at the bottom of the page blank so your head will not drop too low as you read. Since it is awkward to read a sentence that starts on one page and finishes on the next, never break a sentence between two pages. In fact, many speech experts suggest never breaking even a paragraph between two pages. Never staple the pages of a speech; the speaker should be able to slide the page to one side. Finally, many speakers underline key words for vocal emphasis.

Impromptu speaking   When you speak impromptu, you talk on the spur of the moment, without advance preparation. For example, your boss may suddenly ask you to "bring us up to date on a certain project," or a customer may ask you to "explain a certain service." Usually, of course, you will not be asked to make impromptu remarks unless you have some knowledge in the area.

Here are some suggestions to help you in impromptu speaking situations: (1) Anticipate. Try to avoid truly impromptu situations. Guess at the probability of your being called on during discussions, meetings, or interviews. Guess at the topics you might be asked to discuss. (2) Keep your remarks short. Say what you have to say and then stop. Do not ramble on, feeling you must deliver a lengthy lecture. (3) Organize as well as you can. If you have a few seconds, jot down your main points. Stick to them; avoid tangents. (4) Relate to experience. You will speak more easily and confidently if you try to relate the topic to your specific experiences, and to the topics you know best.

6. Media and telecommunications

Besides all the other delivery skills involved in speaking, you must keep in mind certain techniques for dealing with various technologies, such as telephones, radios, television or video cameras, and video teleconferencing. Here are four sets of suggestions for dealing with speaking situations involving media and telecommunications.

Preparing People tend to waste time and miss the chance to get across their main points because they do not prepare adequately. Gather your data in advance: get together any reports, correspondence, and notes you will need for reference. Also, jot down a brief outline of the points you want to cover. This will help you to avoid rambling and forgetting important points or questions. If you are appearing on television or radio, anticipate what questions you may be asked. Just as important, prepare the main points you want to emphasize. For telephone calls, have paper available so you can avoid having to shuffle around during the call if you need to take notes. Date and head all phone-call notes. When you are dealing with less familiar equipment—cameras, microphones, and so on—try to practice in advance with it.

Using audio devices Audio devices include telephones and microphones (for radio, television, video, or video teleconferencing).

1. Speak conversationally Speak using pauses and inflection, as though you were addressing a small group of people. This is especially difficult when your audience is not physically present.
2. Watch your volume and distance Find out if you are using an omnidirectional or a unidirectional microphone. Omnidirectional microphones will pick up sounds equally at all distances; for unidirectional microphones, you must keep your distance (which can vary from two to 20 inches) constant. If you are using a telephone, remember that it is an amplifying instrument; raising your voice will be hard on your listener's ears.
3. Avoid unwanted sounds Audio devices may exaggerate the sound of your breathing, making it sound like gasping and wheezing. To breathe quietly, arch your tongue tightly against your lower teeth. Remember that audio devices will pick up all sounds. Avoid rattling your paper, drumming your fingers, scraping your chair, and jingling coins.

Using cameras   You will use a camera when you are speaking on video, video teleconferencing, or television.

1. *Prepare for mechanical distractions*   Cameras can be disconcerting if you're not used to them. Try to arrive at the studio early enough to get used to them. Rehearse on set to learn cues and see the equipment; rehearse with various camera shots.

2. *Decide where to focus*   Find out in advance whether to look at the camera, at the interviewer, or at the other people present. If you are recording a one-person video, you will probably look directly at the camera; if you are appearing on a talk show, you will probably look at the host; if you are appearing on a video teleconference, you will probably look at the other participants.

3. *Dress appropriately*   In general, dress unobtrusively, especially when you are appearing on television. Generally, that means solid colors—grey, blue, beige. Avoid tweeds, stripes, and patterns that appear to jump around on the screen. Avoid white, which may glare, and black, which absorbs light. Other than a watch or wedding ring, avoid jewelry, especially if it is jangling or otherwise distracting.

Using two-way technology   A technology is called two-way if it enables you to interact with your audience. For example, the telephone and two-way video teleconferences (in which the audience, from a different location, can transmit comments to you) are two-way. On the other hand, one-way technology includes television, radio, video, and one-way video teleconferencing.

1. *Try to establish rapport*   Since you cannot see the other people, visualize them in your mind to increase your ability to empathize with them. Identify yourself clearly, state your reason for speaking, and tie your reason to your audience's benefits. If you are telephoning, find out if you are calling at a convenient time. If you are using other two-way technologies, consider how to appeal to audience members and make them comfortable.

2. *Listen carefully*   Use the listening techniques just described on pages 90–91. In addition, if you are telephoning or using two-way teleconferencing that includes audio interaction only, obviously you will not be able to see nonverbal signs of agreement, disagreement, or uncertainty from your audience; therefore, listen very carefully to vocal inflection. Finally, make sure you understand your receiver by paraphrasing and by summarizing.

III. SELECT YOUR VISUAL AIDS

Once you have prepared what you are going to say—either for a standard presentation or for the other kinds of speaking situations encountered in business—select your visual aids. No matter how well you have prepared what you are going to say, and indeed no matter how skilled you may be in your speaking delivery, your audience has the capacity to think about other things. In part, this capacity is based on their ability to comprehend faster than you can speak.

Therefore, keep them concentrating on your ideas by giving them something to look at, to back up what you're saying. Visual aids increase your audience's comprehension and retention. Seeing something in addition to hearing it is much more effective than either just seeing it or just hearing it. Visuals add interest, variety, and impact—and remain in the memory longer than words.

In most business and professional settings, visual aids of some kind are appropriate. In some situations, however, the group you are addressing may ask you not to use aids, or to use only certain kinds of aids. Naturally, audience considerations should always govern your aid selection.

Once you have met your audience's needs, then, the process of choosing and using effective visual aids includes two steps: (1) compose your visual aid content, and (2) choose your visual aid equipment.

1. Compose your visual aid content

Unfortunately, many people giving managerial presentations get involved with fancy technology or colored graphics that don't communicate anything useful. The best way to compose visual aids is to think about what you are trying to communicate—before you think about the artwork, the computer graphics, or the medium you might use to say it.

The content of your visual aids should have appropriate formality, a necessary function, a main idea and supporting detail, and easy readability.

Appropriate formality   Your first question should always be, "How formal do I want to be on this occasion?"

A *formal* tone results from visual aids created entirely in advance, before the presentation starts. If the occasion is formal, you may use slides, overhead transparencies, or flip charts; the important variable is your having prepared them in advance. Formal aids may be professionally finished, often in many colors. They assure you of a great deal of control over your presentation's content; audience involvement is relatively limited.

A *semiformal* tone comes from creating your aids partially in advance and partially during the presentation. For example, you might prepare part of a chart and then, for a more dramatic effect, write certain numbers as you speak. Or you might have blanks that you will fill with audience responses. A semiformal tone allows you to maintain some control along with some flexibility and spontaneity.

Finally, if you want to establish a more *informal* tone, create your visuals during the presentation itself. You might, for example, choose to write on a blackboard, a flip chart, or even an overhead transparency during the talk. Informal aids are the most flexible and spontaneous; they involve your audience the most, but naturally you exert far less control over their content, and as you write you may waste valuable time.

This kind of analysis sounds simple, but you will often see people having severe problems with visual aids in business presentations because they neglect these considerations. For example, they bring professionally prepared slides into a brainstorming session and seem surprised when people don't participate. Or they scribble hastily on a blackboard and seem surprised when people assume they haven't prepared in advance.

Necessary function After you've decided how formal you want to be, decide what visuals are necessary. Many managerial presentations are clogged with unnecessary visuals—such as a visual every 15 seconds or slides that echo word for word what the presenter is saying. Unnecessary aids are like unnecessary words in writing: get rid of them.

Your visual is necessary only if it fulfills one of two functions: (1) if a word chart, it shows your agenda or main ideas; (2) if a graph, it illustrates relationships.

1. Word charts consist—obviously—of words rather than figures. One kind of word chart is an agenda, or a list of your three to five main points. If you use an agenda chart, always show it at the beginning of the presentation (during your preview)—whether it's on a flip chart, a slide, the board, or even a handout. You may elect to leave the agenda chart showing throughout your presentation and point to it each time you move to a new section. A main-idea or recommendations chart lists your main conclusions. It should be displayed at the beginning of a presentation if your listeners are likely to agree with you, and at the end if they are not likely to agree. Other than agenda and recommendations charts, use word charts only when you think your audience will be lost without one.

Avoid overusing word charts in your presentations. One of the worst so-called visual aids is an outline—or, worse yet, a word-for-word script—of your presentation displayed at the same time you say something. See the following example for a typical ineffective "word script" aid:

INEFFECTIVE VISUAL: "WORD SCRIPT"

This is an ineffective word chart because it is an almost word-for-word script of what you are saying. Word scripts have the following drawbacks:

1. They insult your audience's intelligence by forcing them to read practically word for word what you are saying.
2. They allow your audience to read ahead.
3. They force your audience to read long sentences and to listen at the same time.

---

2. *Graphs* illustrate ideas. They are true visual aids because they actually show something, using design elements rather than just words.

A graph is necessary if it performs one of the following six functions:

If you want to show	Chart to use	Tips
Component parts of one item (contributions, percentages, shares, proportions of one item)	Pie **ENTIRE ITEM** **broken into components**	Arrange with most important component at 12 o'clock; if components are equally important, arrange from smallest to largest. Usually, limit to no more than five components.
Component parts of more than one item (contributions, percentages, shares, proportions of more than one item)	Subdivided bar  SERIES OF ITEMS **broken into components**	Use subdivided bars to show a breakdown of items, because columns imply a time sequence.
	Subdivided column 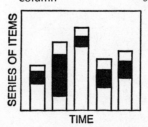	Use columns to show time sequence.

If you want to show	Chart to use	Tips

Rank comparison

(more/less, variation, difference between)

Bar

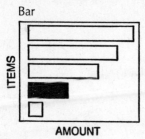

AMOUNT

Arrange in order to suit your needs: alphabetical, low to high, high to low.

Use a bar chart rather than a column chart, which implies a time sequence.

Column

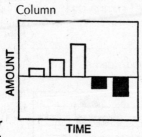

TIME

Use a column chart to emphasize extreme variability or magnitude.

Limit to a small number of time periods or plottings.

Variation over time or frequency distribution

(increases/decreases, changes, trends, concentrations)

Line

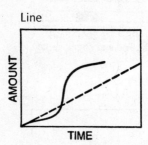

TIME

Use a line chart to emphasize movement or change.

Use for a large number of time periods.

Usually, limit to three lines at most.

If you want to show	Chart to use	Tips

Sequence

(process, organization, line
of command, time stages)

Flow

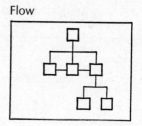

Scatter

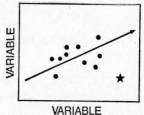

Correlation between items

(relation, increase/
decrease with, change/
vary with)

Paired bar

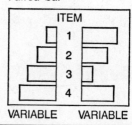

Main idea and supporting detail   Effective visual aids also show both a main idea and supporting detail.

INEFFECTIVE VISUAL: DETAIL ONLY, NO MAIN IDEA

Market share in 1986 was 21%.

INEFFECTIVE VISUAL: MAIN IDEA ONLY, NO DETAIL

Market share has decreased.

EFFECTIVE VISUAL: MAIN IDEA AND SUPPORTING DETAIL

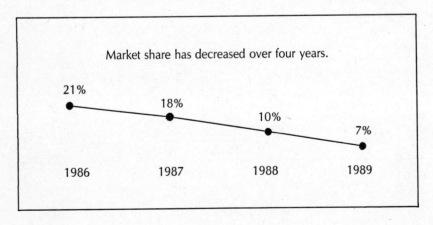

Easy readability If your visual, like a paragraph, includes both a main idea and supporting detail, you don't need to go overboard with design elements. Your audience should think, "What an interesting idea!" or "What interesting data!" not "What spiffy graphics!"

Remember these rules for readability:

1. *Avoid all unnecessary decoration* that does not add to your meaning, such as unnecessary shading, crosshatching, and elaborate coding systems.

2. *Do not overload* your chart with information. In general, include no more than 20 lines of information; avoid overly complex diagrams.

3. *Use clear color coding* If you use colors, do so carefully. Use a consistent color code (such as blue for your main headings throughout). Dark colors (blue, black, red, or green) are easier for the audience to see than washed-out colors (yellow or orange).

4. *Include essential words only* Pare down your words to key words and phrases only. Never give complete sentences. Never, never give complete paragraphs. A visual aid is not the same as a script. Any word important enough to put on a visual is important enough to spell out; avoid mysterious abbreviations.

5. *Make sure your letters are large enough* for your audience to see. This statement sounds embarrassingly obvious, yet overly small lettering is one of the most common problems in visual aids. We cannot establish exact rules of thumb for letter size, because letter size varies with audience size and with projection distance. In general, though, seat yourself in the back row of your audience to check letter size. You may be surprised how large you need to write on a flip chart or blackboard. You may be surprised to see how unreadable typed overhead transparencies are (even if you use primary typeface). *Usually,* the letters on the transparencies themselves should be at least 18-point type for small groups, at least 36-point type for large groups.

6. *Choose a serif typeface* and avoid words made up exclusively of capital letters. Sans-serif type—such as the typeface in the three boxed examples on page 104—is harder to read because the lack of extenders at the edge of each letter, called serifs, leaves the reader's eye with less to "wrap around." All capitals are even harder to read because their equal height, volume, and width give the reader's eye even less to "wrap around." Obviously, then, sans-serif capitals are the hardest letters of all to read; serif lower-case letters—such as the typeface in this paragraph—are the easiest to read.

2. Choose your visual aid equipment

After you have decided on your visual aid content, choose the appropriate equipment. Different kinds of equipment are appropriate on different occasions. For example, in a brainstorming session you would probably choose a chalkboard or a flip chart; professionally produced 35mm slides would defeat the purpose of that kind of occasion. On the other hand, if you were giving a final report, you might choose slides. Again, your communication objective, style, audience, and content—not to mention what equipment is available—should dictate what equipment you choose. Make your choice based on your strategy, not on the technological "bells and whistles." Keeping that caveat in mind, let's examine the three types of equipment available to you.

Animated projection   This includes film and video. Animated projection is useful for showing motion, such as an assembly-line procedure, a skills demonstration, or speeded-up research results.

1. Film   Until the 1980s, film was the major kind of animated projection. Film equipment includes a projector and of course the film itself. Film comes in two different formats, or widths: 16mm and Super 8. Your film projector must be compatible with your film; 16mm film, for example, plays only on a 16mm projector. The more common format is 16mm, because it is more readily available and of superior quality. Super 8 equipment is more compact, travels more easily, and has good quality when projected on a small screen.

2. Video   The second type of animated projection is the videocassette or videodisc. Videos are used for the same purpose as films: to show motion. Their biggest advantage over film is their ability to stop and start. You can interrupt, back-space, or "freeze" a frame to inject comments, ask questions, or answer questions.

Depending on your needs, you may choose one of three video systems. A *television-monitor system* includes a television monitor plus either a videocassette recorder (VCR), which, like an audio tape recorder, both plays back and records, or a videocassette player (VCP), which plays back only. Your audience watches your cassette on the television monitor or monitors. These systems are somewhat portable, and may be moved from room to room on carts. A *large-screen system* includes a video projector and a VCR or VCP. Your audience watches the video on a screen, as they would watch a movie. These projection systems can be portable, but take expert adjustment; some take warm-up time. Usually they are permanently installed, not portable. Finally, a *video recording system* includes a television monitor, a VCR, a camera and tripod, a microphone, and possibly lights. Some recording units, called "camcorders," are light and portable: a battery-operated VCR and camera sit on the camera operator's shoulders. Other recording systems are nonmovable, set up permanently in recording studios.

Videocassettes come in various formats. These include 2-inch or 1-inch "television quality," 3/4-inch "professional quality," and 1/2-inch "home quality." To further complicate matters, there are two separate 1/2-inch formats—Beta and VHS. Furthermore, a 1/4-inch format may be the wave of the future. Generally, the larger the tape's width, the better the quality and the more expensive to produce. Usually, 2- and 1-inch formats are used only by television studios. Most businesses use either 3/4-inch, 1/2-inch Beta, or 1/2-inch VHS. Use 3/4-inch for higher quality and better editing. You'll probably find, however, that 1/2-inch provides sufficient quality for most situations.

The main thing to keep in mind when using video for visual aids is format compatibility. Make sure that the playback unit (VCR or VCP) is the same format as your tape. A tape of any particular width can be played only on a machine designed for that width. For example, a 1/2-inch Beta tape will run only on a 1/2-inch Beta machine. If your tape format differs, either order a different playback unit (VCR or VCP) or have your tape transferred to a different format.

Still projections If you don't need to show motion, you may choose to use still projections, either slides or overhead transparencies. These kinds of projections range from the very formal and prepared to the very informal and spontaneous.

1. *Slides* Slides are most useful when you don't have to write on your visual, or when you are giving a multimedia presentation. One advantage of using slides is that you can select and arrange the sequence yourself, whereas you need special equipment and training to arrange your own animated projections. You can also easily change a slide sequence to suit different audiences. A final advantage is that the projector sits in the back of the room, not blocking anyone's view.

The main disadvantage of slides is the need for a darkened room, which decreases your interaction with your audience. Some new slide projectors, however, work in lighted rooms. Slides are also generally—but not always—more time-consuming and expensive to produce than overhead transparencies.

The most popular size for slides is the 135 slide, usually called the 35mm slide. Other sizes include the Super 8 slide for extremely large images and the less expensive, lesser-quality 126 slide for small images. Slide projectors include a *carousel* on top in which you load the slides. They may also include a zoom lens, which allows you to vary your projected image without having to move your projector. This feature is important if you make presentations in rooms of various sizes. Another possible feature is the remote-control unit (either with or without wires), used to advance, reverse, and focus the slides. A remote control is essential if you're speaking without an assistant. During your presentation you should be standing next to the screen, not by the projector. A host of other features are available for more extravagant slide presentations.

2. Overhead transparencies Sometimes called *acetates* or *foils*, over-heads are quite popular in business presentations. The equipment consists of the transparencies and the projector. The transparencies are usually 8-by-10-inch acetate sheets, often mounted in a plastic or paperboard frame. If you are only going to write on them as you speak, you might use a continuous roll of acetate instead of individual transparencies. To write on the acetate, you also need special acetate pens or grease pencils; regular marking pens won't work.

The main advantage of overheads is their versatility. You can use them informally, writing directly onto the acetate sheet as you face your audience. You can use them semiformally, using a marker to highlight or add information on a partially prepared transparency. Or you can prepare more formal transparencies, from dry-transfer type, from computer-generated type, or from other printed type run through either a special copying machine or a special transparency machine. Overhead transparencies are also easy to use. During your presentation, you place the transparency on the illuminated glass surface of the projector, positioning it so that you can read it (not upside down or backwards). You can also overlay transparencies of additional material, or use a cover-up mask to disclose information progressively.

Overheads also have their drawbacks. They are more awkward to change than slides: instead of the press of a button, you must quickly change them by hand or have an assistant do so. Another drawback is the size of the transparencies. Their 8 × 10-inch format is many times larger than a 2 × 2-inch slide. The main disadvantage is the projector itself. Unlike a slide projector, the overhead projector sits up front—possibly blocking someone's view. For formal presentations in which you don't have to write as you speak, consider slides instead of over-heads—especially if you have access to a machine that doesn't require a darkened room.

Nonprojection visuals   Other visual aids do not involve projection: charts, boards, and handouts.

1. *Charts*   The various kinds of charts include flip charts, cardboard charts, and desk-top charts. The main advantage of all these charts over all projections is the lighting: you can keep the room well illuminated and maintain eye contact with your audience— whether you're showing formal charts prepared in advance or informal charts prepared during the presentation. If you are using pages prepared in advance, remember that most paper is so thin your audience can see through it. Therefore, leave a blank piece between each page. You may also need to leave blank sheets if there are times during your presentation when you don't want any chart showing. The disadvantage of charts is their size: they are quite clumsy to transport.

Chart equipment is far less complex than projection equipment since no electricity or wires are involved. Don't confuse lack of technology with lack of usefulness, however. A flip chart comprises a pad or series of pieces of paper, a stand, and markers. The flip chart paper may be flipped over the stand or ripped off and attached to the wall. A cardboard chart stands alone because it is printed on sturdy cardboard. It may be any size you wish. You need, however, a chalkboard chalk ledge or some other way to stand it up. A desk-top chart is like a miniature flip chart, appropriate only when you are speaking to a very small number of people.

2. *Boards* Like charts, boards have the advantage of being brightly lit; they often elicit the most audience interaction, spontaneity, and flexibility of any kind of equipment. Their main disadvantage is that your back is usually turned toward your audience as you write. (You face the audience when you write on an overhead transparency.)

Boards come in two varieties. Chalkboards are the familiar green or black boards you see in classrooms. The chalk is usually yellow or white, although some presenters use colored chalks effectively. On blackboards, yellow chalk shows up better than white. Plastic boards are made of white plastic, on which you write with special colored markers. They have all the advantages of a chalkboard, without the disadvantage of chalk dust. Regardless of the kind of board you use, always find out how large it is and how to erase it (the plastic boards take special erasers) before you begin.

3. *Handouts* Handouts have one enormous advantage over the other kinds of visual aids: they provide copy your audience can take away with them. They have a huge disadvantage as well: you cannot prevent your audience from reading ahead of you. To overcome that disadvantage, use handouts only in three ways. First, give summary handouts *only* at the end of the presentation; otherwise, your audience will read ahead. Second, use handouts for the very detailed data that your audience must see, but that is too complex to put on a slide or chart. Give these handouts *only* when you get to the point in your presentation when you are discussing the complex data. Finally, you may use handouts to encourage people to take notes. Since you'll give note-taking handouts at the beginning of the presentation, be sure they are vague and general enough so people won't be reading them. An agenda or outline—with plenty of blank space around each item—serves as an effective note-taking handout.

The chart on the following page summarizes advantages and disadvantages of all the types of equipment discussed in this section.

TYPES OF VISUAL AID EQUIPMENT

Equipment	Main advantage(s)	Main disadvantage(s)
Animated projection		
Film	Animated	Dark room; no audience involvement; no "freeze frame"
Video	Animated; can "freeze-frame"; instant development	Formats of all parts of equipment must be compatible (all ¾-inch, all ½-inch VHS, etc.)
Still projections		
Slides	Flexible sequence; projector at back of room	More expensive than overhead slides
Overheads	Flexible sequence; versatile (informal to formal); can face audience while writing	Slightly awkward to manipulate; projector clumsy, may block view
Nonprojection visuals		
Charts	Room brighter; less likely to break down	Clumsy to transport
Boards	Room brighter; may be more spontaneous	Back to audience when you write
Handouts	Can help present summaries or complex data; audience can use for notes	Audience can read ahead

CHECKLIST
SPEAKING: THE PROCESS

I. Prepare your presentation.
   1. Do you have an opening that grabs your audience's attention?
   2. Do you have a preview that outlines your main points, organizational structure, or main objectives?
   3. Do you have a limited number of main points joined by explicit transitions and internal summaries?
   4. Do you have an effective closing that summarizes, refers to your opening, calls for action, or emphasizes audience benefits?

II. Prepare to handle other speaking situations.
   1. Meetings: Have you prepared for both task functions and process functions?
   2. Question-and-answer periods: Have you prepared for when and how to deal with questions?
   3. Listening and discussion sessions: Have you prepared techniques for how to look, feel, think, and speak?
   4. Introductions and team presentations: Have you interested your audience in the topic and the speaker? Have you organized, used clear transitions and consistent visuals, and rehearsed as a team?
   5. Manuscript and impromptu speaking: Is your manuscript speech written in "spoken style" and typed according to the conventions discussed in this chapter? Have you anticipated impromptu situations and decided on techniques for dealing with them?
   6. Media and telecommunications: Have you prepared for the use of various technologies?

III. Select your visual aids.
   1. Visual aid content: Does it have appropriate formality, a necessary function (for word charts and for graphs), a main idea and supporting detail, and easy readability?
   2. Visual aid equipment (film, video, slides, overheads, boards, handouts): Have you kept in mind the advantages and disadvantages of each kind?

OUTLINE
SPEAKING: THE PRODUCT

  I. Practice and arrange.
     1. Practice your presentation.
     2. Make the necessary arrangements.

  II. Relax and gain confidence.
     1. Relaxing physically
     2. Relaxing mentally
     3. Relaxing as you speak

  III. Use your body effectively.
     1. Improve your poise.
     2. Use movement and gestures.
     3. Increase your eye contact.

  IV. Use your voice effectively.
     1. Use effective pitch.
     2. Speak at the correct rate.
     3. Avoid filler words.
     4. Enunciate clearly.

V

SPEAKING:
THE PRODUCT

So far we have looked at the process of preparing a presentation. Most people agree, however, that even a well-organized presentation with effective visual aids can be spoiled by a bad delivery. This chapter, then, looks at the "final product," the physical characteristics you will need in delivering your presentation. It explains how to (1) practice and arrange, (2) relax and gain confidence, (3) use your body effectively, and (4) use your voice effectively.

I. PRACTICE AND ARRANGE

The first step toward effective delivery is to practice and make the necessary arrangements for your presentation.

1. Practice your presentation

Practice is essential for business and professional presentations because such presentations are neither memorized recitations nor word-for-word readings.

Unfortunately, many business and professional speakers neglect this step. But you should remember that it is not enough to have credible content; you must also establish credibility as a speaker. Practicing will allow you to increase your confidence and poise, improve your wording so it flows naturally and spontaneously, identify any flaws or gaps in your speech, deal with distractions, and make sure your visual aids are smoothly integrated into your presentation.

Work from an outline   No one has the time to memorize every business presentation; very few people must read speeches word for word. Therefore, almost all business presentations are best delivered from an outline. With an outline, you will have the assurance that comes from knowing you can refer to notes if necessary. On the other hand, you will avoid both the overreliance and reading problems caused by a word-for-word manuscript and the look of terror of those who attempt to speak with no notes at all.

Writing your outline on 5 × 7- or 4 × 6-inch cards is extremely effective. Of course, you should use any method that is effective for you. However, regular-size paper can be quite awkward to carry and hold, and 3 × 5-inch cards may be too small to fit enough information. Using cards has three main advantages: (1) cards are easy to hold; (2) they allow you to add, subtract, or rearrange your material easily; and (3) they force you to prune your speech down to an outline, so you cannot read it word for word. Print your speech on the cards in outline form; typing is generally too small to read, unless you use a large type. In general, outline at least five minutes' worth of material on each card.

Rehearse Instead of memorizing or reading your speech, become familiar with it by practicing. Rehearse. Out loud. On your feet. With your aids. Timing yourself. Do not practice by sitting at your desk and reading your speech. Stand up and practice aloud. As you do, you may find some of the following rehearsal methods useful.

Some people find it useful to *simulate the situation* in which they will be speaking. One technique is to practice in the exact place you will be speaking. Another is to practice in front of chairs set up as they would be when you give your speech. A final technique is to practice while bouncing a ball (or performing another routine task) to improve your ability to withstand distractions.

You can also work to *improve your delivery* as you practice. One way to do this is to speak into a mirror to improve facial expressions and animation. Or, you might speak into an audio tape recorder to improve vocal expression. Third, try speaking to a friend or colleague, having him or her use the second checklist at the end of this chapter. Best of all, speak in front of a video tape recorder, evaluating the playback with the chapter-end checklist.

A final rehearsal suggestion is to *memorize your opening and closing* only. For longer presentations, memorize your major transitions as well. Good eye contact is crucial for establishing rapport and credibility, so you want to be looking right at your listeners during those important moments. Also, you will feel more confident knowing you will not hesitate during your opening and conclusion.

Practice with your visuals All your work on composing and selecting your visual aids will be wasted unless you use them effectively during the presentation. You don't want to spoil the effect of your aids—not to mention your entire presentation—by a ragged performance along the lines of "How do you turn this thing on?" or "Whoops! Just a minute while I get this set up," or "Sorry about that; I guess the slide is upside down."

First of all, *become familiar* with your equipment. This suggestion sounds so obvious, and yet many speakers have had their entire credibility and confidence undercut because the chart fell over or the projector wouldn't turn on. Practice with your equipment: actually flip the pages, turn on the projector, press the buttons. Make sure you know how to position the slides, insert the cassette, or write large enough. Practice with any given piece of equipment long enough so you can use it casually.

Once you know your equipment, *practice integrating* every visual smoothly into your presentation. Never show a visual aid without explaining what it is and how it ties to what you are saying.

Another aspect of integrating is called "metering out" information—that is, releasing it when, and only when, you want your audience to see it. Always assume your audience will read whatever is in front of them, regardless of what you are saying. They can't help it; they can read faster than you can talk. So don't show them anything until you want them to see it. As examples: don't pass out a long handout at the beginning of your presentation and expect your audience not to read ahead; don't put up a slide with your conclusion visible until you want your audience to see it. With formal aids, you can use a mask (such as a piece of cardboard) to cover up information until you're ready, or use a series of overlays to add information when you want to. With informal aids, write information only as you discuss it. With handouts, be particularly cautious: avoid giving out detailed handouts (this includes perhaps all handouts except agendas) until the end of your presentation.

Smooth integration also involves getting rid of visuals after you're through discussing them. You can easily turn off slides and erase boards. Flip charts are a bit more problematic. Decide in advance what you're going to do: detach pages to post, or flip to blank sheets in between charts. Avoid ripping off sheets and scattering them on the floor.

In addition, smooth integration means paying special attention to two potential delivery problems. First, speak a bit more loudly than usual because speakers tend unknowingly to decrease their volume when they use visuals. Second, keep up your eye contact. Speakers also tend to get so engrossed with their machinery or charts that they forget to look at their audience.

Finally, *practice some special techniques* for certain kinds of visuals. First, if you are writing as you speak, avoid writing too long or talking only to the board. You might draw very faint figures in advance and trace over them during the presentation. Second, if you are using a projector, avoid talking to the screen (a very prevalent problem). If possible, stand next to the screen rather than next to the projector. Third, if you are pointing, face your audience. Use the hand closer to the equipment to avoid putting your back to the audience. Don't use a pointer unless absolutely necessary; if you do use one, avoid fidgeting with it.

2. Make the necessary arrangements for your presentation

Curb any tendency to "let the janitors take care of it" or "let my secretary take care of it." The absence of chairs or of chalk can ruin your credibility. Using the first checklist at the end of this chapter, think through and write explicit instructions for the person who will be making your arrangements; follow through to make sure your instructions are carried out.

Audience notification   To make sure your audience is notified most effectively, think through these four questions. (1) Who? Who, precisely, should be informed? (2) How? Should you speak with people individually (more personal, more flexible, more immediate response), write to them (more formal, less likely to be forgotten), or both? (3) By whom? Should the notification go out under the name of the speaker, an authority figure, a group, a department, a company? (4) What? Exactly what advance information do you want your audience to have?

Room arrangements   Make sure the chairs are arranged appropriately, given the facility, the group size, your communication objective, and the management style you have chosen. In general, use circular, semicircular, or horseshoe configurations to increase participation (e.g., in brainstorming sessions or meetings), and straight lines of chairs with the speaker in front to increase formality (e.g., for lectures or other formal presentations).

You may also need to make other room arrangements. For example, make sure you have enough chairs. On the other hand, get rid of extras before the presentation because people do not like to move once they are seated. Also, check for correct lighting and ventilation. Alleviate distractions as much as possible. Finally, if appropriate, check for pads and pencils, name cards, refreshments, and ashtrays.

Visual aids arrangements   A final set of arrangements has to do with your visual aids. (1) Equipment. Arrange for the projector and screen, including film, cassette, disc, slides, pens, and extension cords. If you are using charts or boards, arrange for stands, paper, pens, chalk, and erasers. Make sure your handouts are ready to go. (2) Visibility. See that your visuals are visible to every person in the audience. (3) Sequence. Your charts, slides, or handouts should be arranged in the correct order.

II. RELAX AND GAIN CONFIDENCE

Even after practicing and arranging presentations, most people have experienced the quivering, fidgeting, shaking, trembling, sweating, stammering, and fluttering associated with stage fright. In fact, a survey quoted in the *Book of Lists* ranks public speaking as Americans' number one fear—ahead of both death and loneliness.

In conversation, most of us feel alert, energetic, natural, confident, and enthusiastic. We can be ourselves, not worrying about our hands or posture, not putting on a false, formal personality. If you can relax as you speak in front of a group, you can be the same kind of speaker you are conversationally.

People relax in different ways. Here, then, are a series of relaxation techniques. Use whichever ones are most useful to you. I have categorized them as methods for relaxing (1) physically, (2) mentally, and (3) as you speak.

1. Relaxing physically

The following techniques are based on the assumption that by relaxing yourself physically you will calm yourself mentally.

1. Relax your entire body   One way to relax is to exercise before a presentation. Many people find that the physical exertion of such activities as calisthenics, jogging, or tennis calms them down. Another technique, developed by psychologist Edmund Jacobson, is called *progressive relaxation*. It involves tensing and relaxing muscle groups. To practice this:

a. Set aside about 20 minutes of undisturbed time.

b. Find a comfortable, darkened place where you can lie down.

c. Tense and relax each of the following muscle groups in turn. To tense a muscle group, clench vigorously for a full five to seven seconds. To relax a muscle group, release the tension very quickly and enjoy the warmth of relaxation. The muscle groups are: hands, arms, forehead, neck and throat, upper back, lower back, chest, stomach, buttocks, thighs, calves, and feet.

d. Repeat the procedure at least twice, tensing and relaxing each group of muscles in turn.

e. Check your body to find if any areas still feel tense; repeat the tense-and-relax cycle in those areas.

2. *Relax specific body parts* For some people, stage fright manifests itself in certain parts of the body—for example, in tensed shoulders, quivering arms, or shaky knees. Here are some exercises for relaxing specific body parts.

   a. Relax your head—and get rid of a choking sensation—by rolling your neck: side to side, front to back, chin to chest, or all the way around.
   b. Relax your shoulders by raising one or both of them as if you were shrugging. Then roll them back, then down, then forward.
   c. Relax your arms and hands with one of two exercises. *Shake-outs* loosen the entire arm. Begin by shaking your arms only at the shoulders. Gradually, shake your arms only at the elbow. Finally, let your hands flop at your wrists. *Fist clenches* release tension in your hands. Start with an open hand and close each finger one by one, making a fist.

3. *Relax your voice* For other people, stage fright manifests itself in the voice. Symptoms include cracking, quivering, and dry mouth. Here are two warm-up exercises for relaxing your voice.

   a. Hum slowly and carefully—never forcing the voice for greater volume. Also, hum with a full range of pitches; this will open up a greater range for you to use when you start speaking.
   b. Practice controlled inhalations and exhalations. The exhalation may be a series of short, staccato bursts of air, or one long, continuous stream of air released as slowly as possible. Throughout the exercise you should focus upon the basics of correct breathing: expanding around the waist when taking a breath, and using the diaphragm (and sheath muscles of the waist) to control the air release and support of the voice.
   c. In addition to vocal warm-up, here are some general suggestions for keeping your voice in shape: (1) Wake up two to three hours before you have to speak. This provides a natural warm-up period for your voice, and also insures that your voice is well rested. (2) Take a hot shower to wake up your voice, or to soothe a tired and irritated set of vocal cords. Steam is very soothing and will help your vocal cords shed any mucus or phlegm that has built up on them. (3) Avoid drinking milk or consuming other dairy products before you speak. Dairy products tend to coat the vocal cords, and this may cause problems during your presentation. (4) Drinking any warm liquid will soothe a tired voice. Ideal candidates are tea and coffee. (5) Sufficient rest is the best guarantee of a good vocal performance.

4. Relax physically at the last minute   The preceding exercises may prove helpful well before your presentation, but obviously you cannot start doing push-ups or practice humming the moment you are about to speak. Fortunately, however, there are techniques you can use to relax your body at the last minute.

   a. Isometric exercises: These involve clenching and then quickly relaxing your muscles. For example, you might press or wiggle your feet against the floor, your hand against your other hand, or your hands against the table or chair; you might clench your fists, thighs, or toes. Then quickly relax whatever muscles you just clenched. No one can see you doing this exercise right before you start to speak.
   b. Deep breathing exercises: These involve inhaling slowly and deeply, then exhaling slowly and completely. Obviously, avoid hyperventilating.

2. Relaxing mentally

Whereas some people prefer methods of physical relaxation, others prefer techniques for mental relaxation. Mental relaxation is based on the assumption that if you calm yourself mentally, all the physical sensations (shaking knees, quivering voice, and so forth) will go away. In other words, for some people the physical follows the mental. Here are five techniques you can use to relax yourself mentally before making a presentation.

1. *Think and act positively*   Base your thinking on the Dale Carnegie argument:

  a. To regulate your thinking, regulate your actions.
  b. To feel brave, act as if you are brave.
  c. To develop courage in front of an audience, act as if you already have it.

2. *Use systematic desensitization techniques*   Through these procedures, developed by psychologist Joseph Wolpe, you force yourself to relax as you imagine or act out a series of successively more anxiety-ridden situations. Complete any one of the relaxation exercises described above before you start the sessions; force yourself to remain physically relaxed during the sessions. Here is a series of four sessions in which you imagine yourself going through the steps of a presentation:

  a. writing a presentation
  b. practicing a presentation
  c. walking to the front of the room
  d. delivering a presentation

Here is a series of four sessions that you might act out with a small group:

  a. reading a presentation aloud
  b. standing in front of the group
  c. reading the presentation in front of the group
  d. speaking in front of the group

3. *Think nonjudgmentally*   Base your thinking on Eastern philosophy. Here I have applied to speaking the advice tennis expert W. Tim Gallwey gives tennis players.

    a. Avoid both positive and negative evaluations of your ability.

    b. Describe your habits (such as "I notice a monotone"; "I see a nervous gesture"); do not evaluate those habits (such as "I have a terrible voice!" "I'm a terrible speaker!").

    c. Instruct yourself by concentrating on a visual image of what you want to look like; do not use word commands (such as "Stand up straight!" "Speak up!").

    d. Trust your body to acquire the desired behavior of the visual image; do not continually castigate yourself for failing.

4. *Think rationally*   Base your thinking on the *rational-emotive* system developed by psychologist Albert Ellis:

    a. Transcend the ABCs of emotional reactions:
        A. Activating Event (such as nervous speaking gestures) sparks a
        B: Belief System (such as "What a disaster!"), which causes
        C: Consequences (such as depression or anxiety)
           by
        D: Disputing irrational Belief Systems with rational thought.

    b. Beware of some common irrational Belief Systems:
        "Everybody must totally approve of everything I do."
        "I must be perfect in every way."
        "It's a terrible catastrophe when something goes wrong."
        "I cannot influence or change my behavior."
        "If I'm not perfect, then I'm terrible."

5. *Relax mentally at the last minute*   Even at the last minute, you may attack stage fright mentally by using what behavioral psychologists call *internal dialogue*, which means, of course, talking to yourself.

    a. Give yourself a pep talk: "What I am about to say is important"; "I am ready"; "They are just people."

    b. Play up your audience's reception: "They are interested in my topic"; "They are a friendly group of people."

    c. Repeat positive phrases: "I'm glad I'm here; I'm glad you're here"; "I know I know"; "I care about you."

3. Relaxing as you speak

Here are three techniques you can use to help you relax even as you begin to speak:

1. Speak to the interested listeners   There are always a few kind souls out there who nod, smile, and generally react favorably. Especially at the beginning of your presentation, look at *them*, not at the people reading, looking out the window, or yawning. Looking at positive listeners will increase your confidence. Soon you will be looking at the people around those good listeners, and then at every person in the audience.

2. Remember that you feel worse than you look   Your nervousness probably is not as apparent to your audience as it is to you. This statement might sound a little too optimistic, so let me back it up with two kinds of evidence. First, having watched thousands of videotapes of managers and students, I'm amazed at the number of them who say, "Hey, I look better than I thought I would!" Second, even trained speech instructors do not see all the nervous symptoms a speaker thinks he or she is exhibiting.

3. Concentrate on the here and now   Think about your content and your audience. Do not allow yourself to think of either past regrets or future uncertainties. Do not analyze what you should be doing. Concentrate completely on communicating information to people.

III. USE YOUR BODY EFFECTIVELY

Once you have practiced and relaxed, you will be set for an effective delivery. Your body language, especially your eye contact and movement, will say a lot about your credibility as a speaker. Unfortunately, many business and professional speakers tend to be overly stiff and formal. To avoid lifeless presentations, check your behavior in each of the following areas: (1) poise, (2) movement/gestures, and (3) eye contact.

1. Improve your poise

Poise means general confidence and lack of tension. The most prevalent poise problems involve posture: standing either too rigidly or too sloppily.

Posture

Do stand:
- in a relaxed, professional manner;
- comfortably upright, with your weight distributed evenly;
- with your feet aligned under your shoulders and neither too close nor too far apart.

Don't stand:
- in an "Attention!" pose;
- in an informal slouch (keeping your weight to one side or swaying from side to side);
- in an ankles-together "reciting schoolchild" stance;
- in a legs-apart "cowpoke straddle."

Dress

Do dress:
- appropriately for the occasion and the audience;
- comfortably and in good taste;
- to project an image consistent with your communication objectives.

Don't dress:
- in clothing that will distract from your message, such as loud ties or showy, dangling jewelry.

Approach (to the speaker's position)

Do approach:
- calmly and unhurriedly;
- with a brief pause for eye contact before launching into your presentation.

2. Use movement and gestures

Movement and gestures include use of your body, your hands and arms, and your face. In general, most speakers find it much easier to avoid nervous gestures than to use good ones. Remember, though, that lively delivery demands some movement, so make an effort to move. It will relieve the visual monotony presented by a stationary speaker, and will release some of your tension and stage fright as well.

Full-body movement

Do move deliberately:
- to change mood or pace;
- to draw attention to and from a visual aid;
- to reinforce an idea (such as making a transition by stepping to the side or emphasizing an important point by leaning forward).

Do not move randomly:
- nervously;
- continually, such as constantly pacing or swaying.

Hand and arm gestures

Do gesture:
- naturally, as you would in conversation;
- to reinforce your content (such as describing a size or shape, emphasizing an important point, enumerating a list, or pointing to a specific item on a visual aid).

Do not move:
- nervously, such as by tugging your ear, scratching your arm, or licking your lips (you will probably find it fairly easy to correct distracting gestures once you know you are using them);
- into one position for too long; especially avoid the "fig leaf" (hands clasped in front), the "parade rest" (hands clasped in back), the "pocket-change jingle," and the "podium clutch";
- with stylized, artificial, unvaried, constantly repeated gestures.

Facial expression

Do maintain:
- a relaxed, animated, conversational facial expression.

Do not maintain:
- a stony, deadpan expression.

3. Increase your eye contact

Eye contact is crucial for establishing rapport with your audience. Eye contact allows you to pick up visual clues about your audience's comprehension and opinions, and allows your audience to feel more of a connection with you.

If you have followed the steps for preparing a presentation outlined in Chapter IV, your presentation will be in outline form, preferably on cards. Preparing this outline will relieve you of the panic that sometimes occurs when a person attempts to deliver a memorized speech. In addition, since you will be speaking from a general outline rather than a prose script, you can look at your audience more frequently.

Eye contact

Do look at:
- the entire group, rather than just one side of the room;
- the key decision-makers in the group;
- good listeners who nod and react.

Do not look at:
- a prepared script, which you read word for word, showing your audience a constant view of the top of your head;
- the middle of the back of the room;
- the ceiling or the floor.

IV. USE YOUR VOICE EFFECTIVELY

Anyone who has heard monotonous, timid-sounding speakers knows how important vocal technique can be. The most important voice characteristics are enthusiasm and energy. I find many business and professional people speak too monotonously, so watch for this tendency as you analyze your voice. Check your vocal technique in each of the following four areas.

1. Use effective pitch

Pitch means your voice's inflection, quality, and volume. The most common pitch problems are lack of inflection and lack of volume.

Inflection

Do speak: • with expressiveness and enthusiasm in your voice.

Do not speak: • in a boring monotone.

Quality

Do speak: • in a warm, pleasant tone.

Do not speak: • in a distracting tone—for example, a tone that is too nasal, too high, too rough, or too whiny.

Volume

Do speak: • audibly.

Do not speak: • too quietly; be aware of this pitfall especially if (1) you are using visual aids, (2) you are a woman, or (3) your volume tends to drop toward the end of your sentences.

2. Speak at the correct rate

Rate, of course, is the speed with which you speak. The rate problems I see most often are speaking too slowly (often associated with speaking too softly) and speaking at a monotonous rate (often associated with unchanging inflection).

Speed

Do speak:
- at the correct speed: slowly enough so you can be understood, quickly enough to maintain energy; varying your rate to avoid droning;
- with effective pauses, such as before or after a key term, to separate items in a series, or to indicate a major break in your thought.

Do not speak:
- too slowly (which may bore your listeners) or too quickly (which may lose them);
- with no pauses or variation in speed.

3. Avoid filler words

Filler words are expressions such as "uh," "er," "um," and "ya know." Everybody uses them occasionally, so don't overreact if you notice a few when you speak. And even if you diagnose a distracting, habitual use of filler words, don't panic: most people find it relatively easy to remedy this problem once they recognize it.

Filler words

Do not use:
- distracting, habitual filler words.

4. Enunciate clearly

Enunciation is the way you pronounce your words. A video or audio tape recording will demonstrate your enunciation.

Enunciation

Do enunciate: • clearly.

Do not: • mumble (which may be associated with talking too quietly);
• use run-on words (which may be caused by talking too quickly);
• drop final consonants, as in "thousan'," "jus'," or "goin'."

CHECKLIST
PRESENTATION ARRANGEMENTS

I. Audience notification
  1. List people to be notified.
  2. Decide how people are to be notified (in writing, in person, by phone, combination).
  3. Decide under whose name or auspices the audience is to be notified.
  4. State information to be included in the notification (including agenda or background material if appropriate).

II. Room arrangement
  1. Sketch chair setup.
  2. Note equipment needs: pads, paper, writing instruments, name cards, and ashtrays.

III. Visual aids arrangements
Note which of the following you will provide, and which your arrangement person will provide.

Projections:

Film projector, films
Videotape player, cassettes/tapes/discs
Slide projector, carousel, slides
Overhead projector, acetate slides, acetate markers

For any projection:

Screen
Extension cords
Spare bulbs

Charts:

Flip chart, paper
Cardboard chart
Desk-top chart

For any chart:

Stand
Pens

Boards:

Chalkboard
Plastic board

For any board:

Chalk or pens
Erasing instrument

Handouts

CHECKLIST
SPEAKING DELIVERY

I. Body
   1. Poise.
      Do you look relaxed and professional?
      Are you standing straight, not rigidly, your weight
         distributed evenly and your feet about six inches apart?
      Are you dressed comfortably and appropriately for the
         occasion and the audience?
      Do you approach the speaker's position calmly and pause
         before starting?
   2. Movement and gestures.
      Do you use deliberate, full-body movement (to change
         mood, draw attention to visual aids, and reinforce ideas)
         and avoid random, nervous movement?
      Do you gesture naturally to reinforce your content, and
         avoid nervous and frozen gestures?
      Do you have an animated facial expression?
   3. Eye contact.
      Do you look at the whole audience?

II. Voice
   1. Pitch.
      Do you speak with expressiveness and enthusiasm?
      Do you speak in a warm, pleasant tone?
      Do you speak loudly enough?
   2. Rate.
      Do you avoid speaking too slowly or too quickly?
      Do you vary your rate and use effective pauses?
   3. Filler words.
      Do you avoid distracting, habitual filler words?
   4. Enunciation.
      Do you pronounce your words clearly?

III. Energy
      Do your body and voice communicate excitement, interest,
         and enthusiasm?

VI

OUTLINE
REFERENCE SECTION

VI

REFERENCE SECTION

Whether you are composing a memo or a report, a presentation or a visual aid, the rules of usage and punctuation remain the same. This chapter is designed to help you check these rules quickly.

I am making two assumptions here. First, I assume you know the basic vocabulary of grammar. So, for example, I will not define a noun. Second, I assume you would prefer short, simple rules—even at the expense of absolute technical accuracy. So, for example, I will call the word *and* a *coordinator*, not a *coordinating conjunction*. In short, I have tried to summarize usage rules for an educated but non-specialized audience.

The chapter contains: (1) definitions of terms, (2) usage rules, (3) punctuation rules, and (4) a bibliography.

I. DEFINITIONS

You will need to understand the following definitions:

1. Sentence parts

Subject: a nominal element that governs the main verb.

> **My boss** tossed the badly written memo into the wastebasket.
> Subject

Verb: an element that conveys what the subject is or does.

> My boss **tossed** the badly written memo into the wastebasket.
>   Verb

Direct object: a nominal element that receives the action conveyed by the verb.

> My boss tossed the **badly written memo** into the wastebasket.
>   Direct Object

Indirect object: a noun or pronoun identifying the party receiving the action, always equivalent to a prepositional phrase beginning with *to* or *for*.

> My boss gave **me** the badly written memo.
>   Indirect Object

Complement: a noun or an adjective that follows a linking verb (usually *be, seem,* or *appear*) and specifies something about the subject of the sentence.

> My boss seems **upset** about the badly written memo.
>   Complement

2. Clauses and phrases

Clause: a group of related words that contains a subject and a verb.

My boss tossed the badly written memo into the wastebasket.
Independent clause: can stand alone as a sentence.

After my boss tossed the badly written memo into the wastebasket, . . .
Subordinate clause: cannot stand alone as a sentence.

Phrase: a group of related words missing either a subject or a verb.

After tossing the badly written memo into the wastebasket, . . .
Verb phrase: does not include a subject.

my angry, frustrated boss
Noun phrase: does not include a verb.

3. Relationships between parts

Coordinate: equal in importance.

My boss tossed the badly written memo into the wastebasket; he shouted, "Write more clearly!"
Coordinate: implies both parts of the sentence (on either side of the semicolon) are equal in importance.

Subordinate: less important.

Shouting "Write more clearly!", my boss tossed the badly written memo into the wastebasket.
Subordinate: implies first part of the sentence (before the comma) is less important.

II. USAGE

---

1. Correct sentences

Do not carelessly write incomplete sentences or write double sentences as if they were a true sentence. An incomplete sentence is called a *fragment*—because it is only a fragment of a sentence. Double sentences are usually called *fused sentences* (or sometimes *run-on sentences* or *comma splices*)—because they are two sentences incorrectly stuck together.

Incomplete sentences: fragments

1. Do not carelessly write a sentence part as if it were a complete sentence.

    Especially during the October buying season.

    Fragment missing a verb

    When the October buying season arrives.

    Fragment with subordinated subject and verb

2. Do use fragments carefully for emphasis, parallelism, and conversational tone.

    Practice your speech thoroughly. Rehearse out loud. On your feet. With your visual aids.

    Fragments used correctly for emphasis

Double sentences: fused sentences (run-on sentences, comma splices)

1. Never stick two sentences together with a comma, a dash, or no punctuation at all.

    The company suffers from financial problems, however, it has great potential in research and development.

    Fused sentences joined by comma

    The company suffers from financial problems——however, it has great potential in research and development.

    Fused sentence joined by dash

    The company suffers from financial problems however, it has great potential in research and development.

    Fused sentence joined by no punctuation

2. Separate fused sentences with a period, a semicolon, or a subordinator.

The company suffers from financial problems. However, it has great potential in research and development.

Separated with period

The company suffers from financial problems; however, it has great potential in research and development.

Separated with semicolon: implies the two clauses are of equal importance.

Although it suffers from financial problems, the company has great potential in research and development.

Subordinated first clause: implies the first clause is less important.

Parallelism Express ideas of equal importance in grammatical structures of equal importance.

1. Parallel adjectives

Wrong: He was *sensitive* and *a big help.*
Right: He was *sensitive* and *helpful.*

2. Parallel nouns

Wrong: The new manager is *a genius, a leader,* and *works hard.*
Right: The new manager is *a genius, a leader,* and *a hard worker.*

3. Parallel verbs

Wrong: The staff should *arrive* on time, *correct* their own mistakes, and *fewer* sick days will be used.
Right: The staff should *arrive* on time, *correct* their own mistakes, and *use* less sick leave.

4. Parallel bullet points

Wrong: The president announced plans to:
- *trim* the overseas staff,
- *cut* the domestic marketing budget, and
- *better* quality control.

Right: The president announced plans to:
- *trim* the overseas staff,
- *cut* the domestic marketing budget, and
- *improve* quality control.

5. Parallel comparisons

Wrong: First *identifying* yourself is more effective than to *start* right off with your sales pitch.

Right: First *identifying* yourself is more effective than *starting* right off with your sales pitch.

6. Parallel repeated words

Wrong: He hands in *his* payroll sheets, *data cards,* and *his* time report on the first of the month.

Right: He hands in *his* payroll sheets, *his* data cards, and *his* time report on the first of the month.

or

He hands in his *payroll sheet* , *data cards,* and *time report* on the first of the month

2. Modifiers

To avoid confusing your reader, place your modifiers as close as possible to the words they modify.

Unclear modifiers   Avoid unclear modifiers.

Unclear: The Task Force seemed sure **on Thursday** the resolution would pass.

Clear: **On Thursday,** the Task Force seemed sure. . . .

Clear: The Task Force seemed sure the resolution would pass **on Thursday.**

Misplaced modifiers   Avoid misplacing a phrase at the beginning of your sentence. An opening phrase must refer to the subject of your independent clause.

Wrong: Young and inexperienced, **the task** seemed easy to Bartholomew. ("The task" is not "young and inexperienced.")

Right: Young and inexperienced, **Bartholomew** thought the task seemed easy.

Wrong: When calling on a client, **negotiation techniques** are important. ("Negotiation techniques" are not "calling on a client.")

Right: **Salespeople** calling on a client will find **negotiation techniques** important.

3. Agreement

Make sure your subject and verb agree. Make sure your pronouns agree with their antecedents.

Subject/verb

1. Make sure your verb agrees with your subject—which may not be the nearest noun.

   The **risks** of a takeover **seem** great.

   The **risk** of a takeover **seems** great.

2. Use the noun nearer the verb to determine the verb for subjects linked by *or* or *nor, either . . . or, neither . . . nor.*

   Either the Art Department **or** the Editorial Department **has** the copy.

3. Use a singular verb for collective nouns, such as *group, family, committee.*

   The committee **is. . . .**

4. Use a singular verb for subjects, such as *each, either, another, anyone, someone, something, one, everybody, no one, nothing.*

   Each of us **is. . . .**

   Another one of the members **has. . . .**

   Either of them **decides. . . .**

Pronoun/antecedent Make sure your pronouns agree with their antecedents.

1. Use a singular pronoun to refer to antecedents such as *person, woman, man, kind, each, either, neither, another, anyone, somebody, one, everybody, no one.*

    Each of the committee members agrees to complete **his** assignment before the next meeting.

    (To avoid possible sexist connotations implicit in the masculine singular pronouns, see page 147 of this book.)

2. Use the noun nearer the verb to determine the pronoun for subjects joined by *or* or *nor.*

    Neither **Cameron** nor **Seth** has completed **his** [not their] memo.

    Either the manager or her **subordinates** have made **their** [not her] group's proposal.

3. Use a singular pronoun for collective nouns.

    The **group** is preparing **its** [not their] statement.

4. Pronoun case

Use the proper case form to show the function of pronouns in a sentence.

CASE FORMS

Subjective	I	he/she	you	we	they	who
Objective	me	him/her	you	us	them	whom
Possessive	my	his/her	yours	our	their	whose
	(mine)	(hers)		(ours)	(theirs)	
Reflexive/	myself	himself/	yourself	ourselves	themselves	
Intensive		herself				

Subjective   Use the subjective case when the pronoun is in the subject. Watch out for:

1. Compound subjects

    He and **I** finished the job. **We** managers finished the job.

2. Subject complements (See the definition of *complement* on page 136.)

    That may be **she.** It was **she who** paid the bill.

Objective   Use the objective case when the pronoun is the sentence object, indirect object, or object of a preposition. Watch out for:

1. Sentence objects

    The auditors finally left **him** and **me.**

2. Prepositions

    Just **between** you and **me** [not *you and I*], . . .

3. *Whom:* Use for the object of the sentence, subordinate clause, or preposition.

    Whom did you contact at ABC Company?

    The new chairperson, **whom** we met at the cocktail party, starts work today.

    For **whom** is the message intended?

Possessive   Use the possessive to show ownership. Watch out for:

Gerunds (*-ing*-ending verbs used as nouns).

We were surprised at **his** [not him] resigning.

Intensive/reflexive   Use the intensive and reflexive for emphasis. Watch out for:

Misuse of *myself*. (Don't use *myself* if you can substitute *I* or *me*.)

Daniel and **I** [not myself] designed the market survey.

He gave the book to Julia and **me** [not myself].

5. Avoiding bias

One of the biggest changes in the business and professional environment has been the increasing effort to alleviate discrimination, as indicated by legislation such as the Civil Rights Act, the Equal Pay Act, and the Rehabilitation Act. Here are some suggestions for avoiding bias in your business and professional communication.

Racism

1. Avoid any word, image, or situation that suggests that all or most members of a racial or ethnic group are the same.

   Anglos: prim, cold, stuffy, rational
   Asians: sinister, inscrutable, serene, industrious
   Blacks: childlike, shuffling, lazy, athletic

2. Avoid qualifiers that reinforce racial stereotypes.

You wouldn't say	So don't say
Anthony, a well-groomed white man, . . .	George, a well-groomed black man, . . .
He's not what you'd call shy. Bob Jones puts on quite a sales presentation.	She's not what you'd call shy. Connie Wang puts on quite a sales presentation.

3. Avoid racial identification except when it is essential to communication.

You wouldn't say	So don't say
Rita, an outgoing white woman, . . .	Sylvia, an outgoing Chicano woman, . . .
Leo McCarthy, noted white legislator, . . .	Willie Brown, noted black legislator, . . .

Sexism

1. Avoid generic terms that imply men are the only people on earth.

Avoid	Prefer
man-made	artificial
man-hours	working hours
workmen's compensation	workers' compensation

2. Avoid job titles that end with the suffix *man*.

Avoid	Prefer
businessman	executive, manager
foreman	supervisor
salesman	sales representative

3. Beware of third-person pronouns. Here are four solutions:

   a. Reword.

Typically, a manager at XYZ Corporation will call monthly meetings with his staff.	Typically, the manager at XYZ Corporation will call monthly staff meetings.

   b. Recast into plural.

Each employee must decide for himself. . . .	Employees must decide for themselves. . . .

   c. Replace with *one, you, he/she, s/he, hers/his.*

his staff	his or her staff

   d. Alternate male and female examples.

4. Avoid sexist salutations, such as *Dear Sirs:* or *Gentlemen.* Here are four alternatives:

   a. Use a descriptive term.

   > Dear Customer:
   > Dear Colleague:
   > Dear Subscriber:

   b. Use a job title.

   > Dear Sales Representative:
   > Dear Permissions Editor:

   c. Use formal asexual salutations.

   > Dear Recipient:
   > Dear Sir/Madam:
   > To Whom It May Concern:

   d. Use informal asexual salutations.

   > Dear Reader:
   > Dear Friend(s):
   > Greetings:

Bias toward the disabled

1. Avoid mentioning an impairment when it is not pertinent.

Avoid	Prefer
The deaf accountant completed the audit.	The accountant completed the audit.

2. Separate the person from the impairment.

Avoid	Prefer
Bob, an epileptic, has no trouble with the new job.	Bob, who has epilepsy, has no trouble with the new job.

3. Avoid using words that would offend you if you were impaired.

Avoid	Prefer
deaf and dumb	hearing- and speech-impaired
fits, spells	seizures, epilepsy
crippled	disabled
spastic/retarded (unless of course, these words are needed to describe a condition precisely)	

III. PUNCTUATION

1. Comma

In general, insert a comma whenever you would have a light, natural pause, or whenever necessary to prevent misunderstanding.

> AND
> BUT
> INDEPENDENT CLAUSE**,** OR   INDEPENDENT CLAUSE**.**
> NOR
> FOR
>
> A long independent clause like this one is perfectly fine**,** but you need a comma before this coordinator and the second independent clause.

> INTRODUCTORY ELEMENT**,** INDEPENDENT CLAUSE**.**
>
> If you find that you have a fairly long introductory element at the beginning of your sentence**,** use a comma before your independent clause.
>
> In addition**,** use a comma after an introductory transition (such as *for example***,** *in the second place***,** *however*).

> ITEM**,** ITEM**,** AND ITEM
>
> Use a comma to separate a parallel series of words**,** phrases**,** or subordinate clauses.

> **,**NONESSENTIAL ELEMENT**,**
>
> Incidental information in the middle of your sentence**,** like this**,** should be set off with commas.
>
> Midsentence transitions**,** moreover**,** are enclosed in commas.

2. Semicolon

Use the semicolon as a period between two closely related independent clauses of equal importance. Do not use the semicolon to separate items in a list unless the list is complex.

INDEPENDENT CLAUSE; INDEPENDENT CLAUSE.

A semicolon indicates a close connection between two independent clauses of equal importance; these clauses will not be joined in addition by a coordinator (*and, but, or, nor, for*).

INDEPENDENT CLAUSE; TRANSITION,
INDEPENDENT CLAUSE.

A semicolon indicates a close connection between two independent clauses of equal importance; however, don't forget the use of the semicolon to separate independent clauses with a transitional word between them (like *however* in this sentence).

ITEM 1A, ITEM 1B; ITEM 2A, ITEM 2B;
ITEM 3A, ITEM 3B.

Use a semicolon to separate items in a series when your list is complex, containing internal commas; when you need stronger punctuation, in order to show where the stronger breaks are; and when you want to avoid confusing your readers, who might get lost with only commas to guide them.

3. Colon

Use the colon as an "introducer" to what follows, as an amplifier of an independent clause, and as a mark of separation.

INTRODUCTION: LIST, SERIES, QUOTE, OR STATEMENT.

Use a colon to introduce the following: a list, a series, a quotation, or a statement.

INDEPENDENT CLAUSE: AMPLIFYING INDEPENDENT CLAUSE.

Often, writers use colons in this way: they separate two independent clauses, of which the second amplifies the first.

SEPARATION: SEPARATION

The colon acts as a separator between each of the following four pairs: a salutation and the rest of the letter, a title and a subtitle, a chapter and verse of the Bible, and the hour and the minute.

4. Dash

Use the dash where you would use a comma, but when you want a stronger—more emphatic—break. Do not use a dash in place of a period or in place of a semicolon between two independent clauses.

—EMPHATIC SUMMARY.
—EMPHATIC PARENTHETICAL REMARK—

Use a dash to emphasize interruptions, informal breaks in thought, or parenthetical remarks—all of which are strong or contain internal commas.

Type a dash- -with no spaces before or after the surrounding words- - as two hyphens.

---

5. Parentheses

Unlike dashes—which emphasize the importance of what they surround—parentheses minimize the importance (of what they surround).

(UNEMPHATIC PARENTHETICAL REMARK**)**

Use parentheses for interruptions or subordinate ideas **(**when you wish the punctuation to be less emphatic than a dash**)**.

TERM (DEFINITION**)**

Parentheses are useful when you are defining a new term or new abbreviation **(**a word or expression that has a precisely limited meaning**)**.

(NUMERAL**)** OR **(**FIGURE**)**

Parentheses enclose enumerators within a sentence, such as **(**1**)** letters and **(**2**)** numbers.

(PUNCTUATING AROUND PARENTHESES**)**

Use these printing conventions:

1. **(**If an entire sentence is within the parentheses, like this sentence, place the period inside too.**)**
2. If just part of the sentence is within the parentheses, as in this sentence, place the period or comma outside the parentheses **(**not inside**)**.

6. Apostrophe

Use the apostrophe to show a noun's or a pronoun's ownership, omissions or contractions, and abbreviations.

NOUN'S OR PRONOUN'S

Use an apostrophe to show a noun's or a pronoun's ownership.

1. For plural or singular nouns or pronouns not ending in an *s* or *z* sound, add the apostrophe and *s:*

    Smith's account
    women's rights
    one's own

2. For plural nouns and pronouns ending in an *s* or *z* sound, add only the apostrophe:

    the Smiths' account
    four dollars' worth

3. For singular nouns and pronouns ending in an *s* or *z* sound, add the apostrophe and *s:*

    my boss's office

4. For hyphenated compounds, use an apostrophe in the last word only:

    my mother-in-law's idea

5. Differentiate between individual and group possession:

    Smith and Green's account [joint ownership]
    Smith's and Green's accounts [individual ownership]

OMISSIONS 'N CONTRACTIONS

Use an apostrophe to mark omissions in contractions.

they are   they're
fiscal 1995   fiscal '95

lowercase letter*'*s
a.b.b.r.e.v.*'*s

When needed: CAPITAL LETTER*'*s
abbrev*'*s
word*'*s (referred to as a word)

Use an apostrophe and *s* to form the plural of lowercase letters and of abbreviations followed by periods. When needed to prevent confusion, use the apostrophe and *s* to form the plural of capital letters and abbreviations not followed by periods.

b*'*s
p.s.*'*s
Ph.D.*'*s
J*'*s

Do not use an apostrophe with the pronouns *his, its, ours, yours, theirs,* and *whose,* or with nonpossessive plural nouns.

> Their department contributed the financial data; **ours** [not our's] added the artwork.

Do not confuse *its* with *it's,* or *whose* with *who's.*

> **Its** filing system is antiquated. [*Its filing system* = *The filing system of it*]
>
> **It's** an antiquated filing system. [*It's* = *It is*]
>
> She is an accountant **whose** results are reliable. [*Whose results* = *the results of whom*]
>
> She is an accountant **who's** reliable. [*Who's* = *who is*]

7. Quotation marks

Use double quotation marks for direct quotations, dialogue, minor titles, and words used specially. Use single quotation marks only for a quotation or minor title within a quotation. Do not use quotation marks for common nicknames, bits of humor, or trite or well-known expressions.

"DIRECT QUOTATION"
"DIALOGUE OR CONVERSATION"
"MINOR TITLES"
"WORDS USED IN A SPECIAL SENSE"

Use quotation marks to:

1. set off all direct quotations (long prose quotations—more than ten lines—are usually set off by single spacing and indentation and lack quotation marks unless these appear in the original);
2. set off dialogue or conversation (with each person's speech as a separate paragraph);
3. set off minor titles (short stories, essays, short poems, songs, articles from periodicals) and subdivisions of books;
4. enclose words used in a special sense or referred to as words.

"PUNCTUATING AROUND QUOTATION MARKS"

Use these printing conventions:

1. Always place the period and comma within the quotation marks.
2. Always place the colon and semicolon outside the quotation marks.
3. Place the dash, the question mark, and the exclamation point within the quotation marks when they apply only to the quoted matter; place them outside when they apply to the whole sentence.

On Tuesday he said, "This idea stinks!"
[punctuation refers to quoted matter only]

When he called on Thursday and said "I've changed my mind; this idea is okay," I was shocked!
[punctuation refers to whole sentence]

> 'QUOTATION WITHIN QUOTATION'
> 'MINOR TITLE WITHIN QUOTATION'
>
> "Use single quotation marks when you have a quotation within a quotation, 'like this.' "
>
> "Use single quotation marks when you have a minor title within a quotation, such as 'The Star-Spangled Banner' in this quoted sentence."

8. Other punctuation marks

Period   Use to:
1. mark the end of declarative sentences;
2. mark most abbreviations;
3. indicate omissions of words in a quoted passage (three or four spaced periods, called an *ellipsis mark*, are used).

Question mark   Use after direct questions.

Exclamation point   Use sparingly to express strong emotion.

Brackets   Use to:
1. set off editorial corrections or interruptions in a quoted passage;
2. replace parentheses within parentheses.

Italics (underlining)   Use for:
1. titles of separate publications (books, magazines, newspapers, long musical works) and titles of plays, films, and long poems;
2. unusual foreign words;
3. words, letters, or figures (numbers) referred to as such;
4. emphasis (use sparingly).

IV. BIBLIOGRAPHY

I have gathered materials from many sources. This bibliography serves both to acknowledge those sources and to provide you with some excellent references for additional reading. The bibliography is purposely short: rather than including every reference for each of the subjects, I selected a few that are useful for business and professional communicators.

Introduction

This part of the bibliography includes analyses that provide overwhelming evidence of the crucial importance of communication for managers, in terms of both time and career advancement.

BOWMAN, G., "What Helps or Harms Promotability?" *Harvard Business Review*, 42 (January–February 1964), 6–26.

CONNELLY, F., ed., "Accreditation Research Project," *AACSB Bulletin*, 15 (Winter 1980), 12–15.

DRUCKER, P., *The Practice of Management*, Chapter 27. New York: Harper, 1954.

EDGE, A., and R. GREENWOOD, "How Managers Rank Knowledge, Skills and Attributes Possessed by Business Administration Graduates," *AACSB Bulletin*, 11 (October 1974), 30–34.

EVANGELAUF, J., "Business Schools Urged to Alter Curricula, Train Managers to Cope with Change," *The Chronicle of Higher Education*, 30 (May 22, 1985), 1.

HILDEBRANDT, H., et al., "An Executive Appraisal of Courses Which Best Prepare One for General Management," *The Journal of Business Communication*, 19 (Winter 1982), 5–15.

KIECHEL, W., "Harvard Business School Restudies Itself," *Fortune*, 99 (June 18, 1979), 48–58.

LIVINGSTON, S., "The Myth of the Well-Educated Manager," *Harvard Business Review*, 49 (January–February 1971), 79–89.

Management and Management Education in a World of Changing Expectations. Washington, D.C.: American Assembly of Collegiate Schools of Business, 1979; Brussels: European Foundation for Management Development Publications, 1980.

Managers for the XXI Century: Their Education and Development. Report of the annual meeting of the American Assembly of Collegiate Schools of Business, Chicago, June 11–13, 1980. St. Louis: AACSB, 1980.

MINTZBERG, H., "The Manager's Job: Folklore or Fact," *Harvard Business Review*, 53 (July–August 1975), 49–61.

SAYLES, L., *Managerial Behavior*. New York: McGraw-Hill, 1964.

Chapter I: Communication strategy

This part of the bibliography includes information on the various aspects of communication strategy outlined in Chapter I.

BETTINGHAUS, E., *Persuasive Communication*, 3rd ed. New York: Holt, Rinehart & Winston, 1980.

BLAKE, R., and J. MOUTON, *The New Managerial Grid*. Houston: Gulf Publishing Company, 1978.

BOETINGER, H. M., *Moving Mountains or the Art and Craft of Letting Others See Things Your Way*. New York: Macmillan, 1969.

DE MARE, G., *Communicating at the Top: What You Need to Know About Communicating to Run an Organization*. New York: John Wiley, 1979.

FRENCH, J., and B. RAVEN, "The Bases of Social Power," in *Studies in Social Power*, ed. D. Cartwright. Ann Arbor: University of Michigan Press, 1959.

IMUNDO, L., *The Effective Supervisor's Handbook*. New York: AMACOM, 1980.

KARRAS, C., and W. GLASSER, *Both-Win Management: How to Work With Your Employees*. Philadelphia: Lippincott, 1980.

KOTTER, J., *Power and Dependence*. New York: AMACOM, 1979.

LEAVITT, H., *Managerial Psychology*, 4th ed. Chicago: University of Chicago Press, 1978.

———L. PONDY, and D. BOJE, eds., *Readings in Managerial Psychology*, 3rd ed. Chicago: University of Chicago Press, 1980.

LIKERT, R., *The Human Organization*. New York: McGraw-Hill, 1967.

SCHEIN, E., *Organizational Psychology*, 3rd ed. Englewood Cliffs, N.J.: Prentice-Hall, 1980.

SIMON, H., *Administrative Behavior*. New York: Free Press, 1976.

TANNENBAUM, R., and W. SCHMIDT, "How to Choose a Leadership Pattern," *Harvard Business Review*, 36 (March–April 1958), 95–101.

VROOM, V., and P. YETTON, *Leadership and Decision-Making*. Pittsburgh: University of Pittsburgh Press, 1973.

Chapters II and III: Writing

This part of the bibliography includes information on both the writing process and the written product.

BERKE, J., *Twenty Questions for the Writer*, 3rd ed. New York: Harcourt Brace Jovanovich, Inc., 1981.

EWING, D. W., *Writing for Results in Business, Government, the Sciences and the Professions*, 2nd ed. New York: John Wiley, 1979.

FIELDEN, J., "What Do You Mean I Can't Write?" *Harvard Business Review*, 43 (May–June 1964), 144–56.

FLESCH, R., *The Art of Readable Writing*, rev. ed. New York: Harper & Row, Pub., 1974.

FLOWER, L., *Problem-Solving Strategies for Writing*. New York: Harcourt Brace Jovanovich, Inc., 1981.

LANHAM, R., *Revising Business Prose*. New York: Scribner's, 1981.

MACK, K., and E. SKJEI, *Overcoming Writing Blocks*. Los Angeles: J.P. Tarcher, 1979.

MINTO, B., *The Pyramid Principle: Logic in Writing*, 2nd ed. London: Minto International, Inc., 1978.

NEWMAN, E., *Strictly Speaking*. New York: Warner Books, 1975.

ORWELL, G., "Politics and the English Language," *Horizon*, 76 (April 1946), p. 252.

ROBBINS, L., *The Business of Writing and Speaking*. New York: McGraw-Hill, 1985.

SAFIRE, W., *On Language*. New York: Times Books, 1981.

SPARROW, W. K., AND D. CUNNINGHAM, eds. *The Practical Craft: Reading for Business and Technical Writers*. Boston: Houghton Mifflin, 1978.

STRUNK, W., and E. B. WHITE, *The Elements of Style*, 3rd ed. New York: Macmillan, 1979.

WYDICK, R., "Plain English for Lawyers," *California Law Review*, 66 (1978), 727–65.

ZINSSER, W., *On Writing Well*, 2nd ed. New York: Harper & Row, Pub., 1980.

_____*Writing with a Word Processor*. New York: Harper & Row, Pub., 1983.

Chapters IV and V: Speaking

This part of the bibliography includes information on how to prepare your remarks, select visual aids, and relax to improve your delivery.

ANDERSON, V., *Training the Speaking Voice*, 3rd ed. New York: Oxford University Press, 1976.

ARGENTI, P., *Note on Oral and Physical Relaxation Skills*. Hanover, N.H.: Amos Tuck School of Business, 1984.

CARNEGIE, D., *Public Speaking and Influencing Men* (sic) *in Business*. New York: Association Press, 1926.

COOPER, K., *Nonverbal Communication for Business Success*. New York: AMACOM, 1979.

GALLWEY, W. T., *The Inner Game of Tennis*. New York: Bantam, 1974.

GLATTHORN, A., and H. ADAMS, *Listening Your Way to Management Success*. Glenview, Ill.: Scott, Foresman, 1983.

JACOBSON, E., *You Must Relax*, 5th ed. New York: McGraw-Hill, 1976.

JAY, A., *Effective Presentation*. London: British Institute of Management Foundation, 1979.

KNAPP, M., *Essentials of Nonverbal Communication*. New York: Holt, Rinehart and Winston, 1980.

MEUSE, L., *Making Business and Technical Presentations*. Boston: CBI Publishers, 1980.

MONROE, A., and D. EHNINGER, *Principles of Speech Communication*, 8th ed. Glenview, Ill.: Scott, Foresman, 1980.

MUNTER, M., "How to Conduct a Successful Media Interview," *California Management Review*, 25 (Summer 1983), 143–50.

REHE, R., *Typography: How to Make It Most Legible*. Carmel, Ind.: Design Research International, 1974.

SCOPEC, E., *Business and Professional Speaking*. Englewood Cliffs, N.J.: Prentice-Hall, 1983.

THRASH, A., A. SHELBY, and J. TARVER, *Speaking Up Successfully*. New York: Holt, Rinehart and Winston, 1984.

TUFTE, E., *The Visual Display of Quantitative Information*. Cheshire, Conn.: Graphics Press, 1983.

WHITE, J., *Using Charts and Graphs*. New York: R. R. Bowker, 1984.

WOLPE, J., *The Practice of Behavior Theory*, 3rd ed. Elmsford, N.Y.: Pergamon Press, 1982.

ZELAZNY, G., *Say It With Charts*. Homewood, Ill.: Dow Jones–Irwin, 1985.

Chapter VI: Reference

This final part of the bibliography includes reference materials on improving grammar, avoiding bias, and documenting research sources.

BERNSTEIN, T., *The Careful Writer*. New York: Atheneum, 1982.

BRUSAW, C., G. ALRED, and W. OLIU, *The Business Writer's Handbook*, 2nd ed. New York: St. Martin's Press, 1982.

The Chicago Manual of Style, 13th ed. Chicago: University of Chicago Press, 1982.

HODGES, J., and M. WHITTEN, *Harbrace College Handbook*, 9th ed. New York: Harcourt Brace Jovanovich, Inc., 1982.

MOYER, R., E. STEVENS, and R. SWITZER, *The Research and Report Handbook for Business, Industry, and Government*. New York: John Wiley, 1981. (Includes lists of sources and specifications for documentation.)

PICKENS, J., ed., *Without Bias: A Guidebook for Nondiscriminatory Communication*, 2nd ed. New York: John Wiley, 1982.

THOMSON, A., and A. MARTINET, *A Practical English Grammar*, 3rd ed. Oxford: Oxford University Press, 1980.

INDEX